A Five-Second Prayer

Ten Words to Redeem Your Soul

Dr. Ella L. Gates-Mahmoud

PAGE PUBLISHING
Conneaut Lake, PA

First originally published by Page Publishing 2024

ISBN 979-8-89315-540-2 (pbk)
ISBN 979-8-89553-293-5 (hc)
ISBN 979-8-89315-564-8 (digital)

Printed in the United States of America

Contents

Dedication

It is with a humble and grateful heart that I dedicate this book on prayer to all the strong, faithful, and courageous people in my life, beginning with my father (the late Gene Arthur Gates Sr.) and, the heroic and steadfast woman in my life, my mother (the late Odessa Holliday-Gates), who both worked tirelessly to ensure the longevity of not just a family but a culture of a people. My mother specifically emphasized the love of dogs, morning glory flowers, and wandering Jew plants. Through my parent's prayers, partnership, and commitment toward life, I learned the value of all life—plants, animals, and humans. They also taught me that being in this society will be a lifelong struggle because, unfortunately, it is not designed to value the lives of all people and that praying people are people preparing for change.

I also want to dedicate this work to my husband, Mr. Eric Yusef Mahmoud, who has exemplified what caring and supportive looks like. My husband is of the Islamic faith, and I've watched him pray several times a day for nearly forty years. I have witnessed him risk his life on numerous occasions for the sake and sanctity of our community. He has modeled for countless all the qualities that will make them worthy and meaningful and how one should respect and honor oneself. It is faith in a higher power that has kept us bonded.

Lastly, I want to dedicate this book to my heirs; I hope one day they will find this book on prayer consequential and something they can use to continue to make the world a better place for all: human, animal, and plant lives.

I want to dedicate the full content of this book on prayer to the memory of my immediate family—all of whom are resting in paradise: my mother, Odessa; my father, Gene Senior; and my three brothers, Willie Senior, Gene Junior, and James. Although they are all gone from this earth, they continuously live on in my heart and soul. I miss them all immensely.

Acknowledgments

To whom much is given, much is required!

—Luke 12:48

This quote reminds me that God has given me so much throughout my life, and I must be compelled to reciprocate my gifts by being a giver as well. That's what my life has been—my gift of service and gratitude. The knowledge and experiences I've gained over my life are immeasurable. Each person I was blessed to encounter over my life has helped provide me with many life lessons and ultimately helped me to stay focused and committed to my purpose for being on this earth. I want to express my gratitude to my incredible family: my husband, Eric Mahmoud; my children Lakesha Odessa Mahmoud-Hunter (husband, Johnny Hunter II), E. Riza Mahmoud (Becky Skiba), C. Quadir Mahmoud (Delondra Baker), Ella Odessa-Faye Gates, Willie Gates Jr., and Samantha Millbrook; and all my grand-children, nieces, nephews, and other family members (too many to name). Your love for me does not go unnoticed or unappreciated.

With everlasting love and respect!

Preface

Why a book on prayer? What difference will it make? These are questions I've asked myself for years until I went to Jerusalem in the summer of 2023—the same summer this Holy Land was terrorized. I hadn't returned to the United States for a week before my joy turned into sorrow. I took and posted hundreds of photos of many historical sites as I walked down the narrow stone streets, where my Lord and Savior, Jesus Christ, surrendered his life on a wooden cross, when I put my feet in the Jordan River where Jesus was baptized by the prophet John the Baptist, and where I posted a handwritten note (prayer) to God into the cracks of the Western Wall, a Jewish holy site in the Old City of Jerusalem.

The prayer read:

Keep me and my entire bloodline healthy, safe, and prosperous.
Keep my mind, body, and spirit stayed upon
your goodness, mercy, and love.
Forgive me for all my sins and fears.
Thank you for my life.
Amen.

I've been preparing, fasting, praying, and saving for years, believing that my pilgrimage to this holy place had to have some type of meaning for my life. This book is the outcome of that experience. What I have come to understand, more so now than ever before, is that prayer has always found a way to bring my troubled spirit a form of peace that I can't understand and a sense of calm and resolution even now as Jews (of Israel) and Muslims (of Palestine) continue to fight for what they believe in this Holy Land.

As a teenager, I contemplated suicide; and with the help, support, and guidance of so many people in my life, I was able to be restored. One way I regained a sense of purpose was by developing a simple prayer to say to myself when I feel like I need to be recentered, and that is what this book is—that simple little prayer that has sustained me for decades of my life and one I hope that will bring some form of hope to others who read this book on the power of prayer for their life.

God, forgive me.
Cleanse me.
Make me whole again.
Amen.

Prologue

"Take her home and make sure she's comfortable," urged the doctors whom my parents had anxiously waited to see for hours and the unqualified midwife who remained perplexed about how to address my ailment. They offered neither a treatment plan nor a diagnosis.

My parents, young and in love, tied the knot during their teenage years. They were both born and raised as sharecroppers on Frank Whitaker's Plantation in Aberdeen, Mississippi. Picture this place they fondly called County Road Number Eight—a long, unpaved rural route winding through cotton, corn, and soybean fields sprinkled with one-room shacks. It stretched from the depths of the woods to the city limits, like a living relic of the bygone days of slavery. Life in this neck of the woods was a real sojourn, as the folks there tell it. The demands of farming left little time for hitting the books. Mom proudly finished her eighth-grade education, but Dad's academic journey stalled in the third grade. Together, they had a family of six, but sadly, two of our siblings didn't make it past childbirth. That left us, the Fab Four—my older brother, yours indeed as the second in line, and our two younger brothers—ready to take on the world.

I came into this world under peculiar circumstances, relying on nothing more than hope and prayer. From the moment I was born, I was afflicted with an undiagnosed blood disorder that left me blind and persistently swollen. My father later shared with me the remarkable story of my healing. I am grateful God had me make it through. I say so because after weeks of my condition deteriorating, my father took me for divine intervention.

In our small country town, Springtime Revivals were a common occurrence. One evening, after a grueling day in the cotton fields that stretched from dawn till dusk (literally twelve or more hours), my father wrapped my fragile, swollen, and feverish body in an old flour sack—baby blankets were a luxury they couldn't afford in those days. Carrying me, lifeless and burning with fever, he made his way to an old, weathered church building hidden deep within the woods. Inside, the preacher was in the middle of a fervent sermon, with deacons kneeling on the moaning bench. The atmosphere was electric, with people around the church experiencing intense spiritual moments—some fainting and others crying out and falling like timber trees freshly chopped down.

My dad, tears streaming down his face, acted independently, not seeking permission or guidance. He gently laid my fragile body on the altar, and the church fell silent, as quiet as the night itself. He knelt at the altar, and with his distinctive Southern dialect and broken English, he cried out, *"My baby's swollen and blind. The doctors have given up on her. Please, pray for my child."* Without hesitation, an elderly minister asked the congregation to extend their hands toward my lifeless form as he began to pray. My father described feeling overwhelmed as the minister offered his prayer, and those around him touched him, their voices raised in cries and pleas to God for some semblance of a miracle.

"My knees were trembling on that moaning bench, and as I gazed up at you lying on that altar, I witnessed something truly miraculous. You began to move, a sight I hadn't seen in weeks. Overwhelmed with emotion, I jumped to my feet, and my eyes filled with disbelief. You were turning your head from side to side as though you were gazing at the very lights that lit up the church ceiling," my father recounted with a heart brimming with joy and gratitude.

The preacher addressed the congregation with a powerful proclamation: *"She has been healed. By his stripes, she has received healing."*

Chapter 1

Receiving a "death notice" is a surreal experience, and I've had that bitter taste twice in my life. Never did I fathom that I'd be walking through the valley of the shadow of death once more. After all I'd endured since birth, I believed I'd already carried my fair share of suffering. So, when the doctor delivered the shattering news of a life-threatening cancerous tumor, it rattled me to the core in a way I never thought I would encounter.

My husband asked, *"What stage are we dealing with?"*

I sat there, immobilized, my heart racing at a dizzying speed.

The doctor took a deep breath before delivering the verdict. *"It's stage three."*

My heart seemed to halt, and I struggled to catch my breath. *"How many stages are there?"* I managed to ask.

His response, *"Four,"* felt like another blow, stealing the air from my lungs.

I couldn't contain my tears, and through my sobs, I overheard my husband and the doctor discussing the situation. The only thing I recall after that was the doctor saying, *"My office will reach out to you next week to discuss treatment options."*

Rewinding…

It is 2005. I, Ella Gates-Mahmoud, age forty-five, am living the prime years of my life and career.

I had gone in for a routine Pap smear exam, and my doctor noticed something unusual.

"I couldn't advance the instrument past a certain point. You will need to return for a follow-up examination, which will require sedation," stated the doctor.

So I went to the next appointment with my husband, and after the procedure, when I regained consciousness, the doctor conveyed the news to both my husband and me.

"A tumor was responsible for the blockage. I will go ahead and conduct a biopsy. If there is anything that you should be concerned about, a specialist from another department will contact you," informed my doctor.

Several days later, a specialist from the women's clinic at the University of Minnesota Hospital eventually called me in for a follow-up discussion regarding the Pap exam. My husband and I walked into the clinic, uncertain about what he would say. After some small talk, a young Black male doctor settled into his chair and looked into my eyes; and from the gravity of his expression, I could sense that something was deeply amiss. He seemed to have tears in his eyes, and before he spoke, my stomach seemed to plummet, and it felt like the air was escaping from my lungs. My heart raced, and I was utterly frozen. He whispered as gently as he could, *"The tumor that caused the blockage is cancerous."*

The room seemed to whirl around me, and I felt lifted off the ground. I was overwhelmed with every emotion one could feel: devastation, shock, or unbelief. Moreover, when we returned home, my husband was silent throughout, perhaps because of helplessness because for as long as I have known him, he had never seemed so powerless as much as he did at this moment. I had always seen him in control, but this time, he wasn't!

During this time, my husband and I had adopted three children: two sons and a daughter. My sons, now in their twenties, chose to stay their distance. I'm not entirely sure of their reasons, but I suspect they had come to terms with the idea of my impending mortality and weren't quite sure how to handle it. On the other hand, my eldest daughter drew closer to me. She visited and called more frequently, providing additional comfort and support.

It was not long after my initial diagnosis that I sought a second opinion. This was from the Mayo Clinic in Rochester, Minnesota, where the doctor confirmed the diagnosis and presented me with treatment options: chemo or radiation. My choice leaned toward radiation, not because one method was necessarily more effective than the other, but in part because I was apprehensive about losing my hair. I underwent several rounds of radiation, and fortunately, I didn't experience any adverse effects. Surprisingly, I remained relatively healthy during this period. Additionally, I opted for a total hysterectomy, sparing the doctor the challenge of shrinking the tumor. I felt a deep sense of gratitude that the cancer had stayed localized within the tumor and hadn't spread to other organs or parts of my body.

My contentment about my decision to pursue treatment wasn't solely because I didn't experience adverse effects. Many individuals are plagued by regret when in the throes of treatment. Surprisingly, that sentiment never once crossed my mind. I had unwavering trust that God had placed the right doctors with the necessary expertise and experience in my path. While my faith remained steadfast, I also firmly believed that God orchestrates the presence of people in our lives, including doctors, for a purpose. In fact, I still possess a picture of the cancerous tumor that was removed from my body, and from time to time, I gaze upon it. It serves as a poignant reminder of God's grace in my life and doctors' role in restoring my health.

Nonetheless, like every story, mine has an interesting twist too. My surgery on the tumor was a resounding success, but the real challenge came when I attempted to get up and walk to the bathroom afterward. My legs gave way, and I initially assumed it was just post-surgery weakness. I couldn't have been more wrong. The doctor promptly arranged for a full-body CAT scan right from my bed, and it revealed the grim truth—my left leg was paralyzed. The reason behind this unforeseen complication was quite unusual.

The University of Minnesota hospital and clinics serve as a "learning center for medical students," allowing them to perform procedures while the overseeing doctor observes. In my case, a medical student had inadvertently clamped down on my femoral nerve during the surgery, affecting the mobility of my left leg. Several hours with restricted blood flow had caused the paralysis. Thankfully, the nerve wasn't severed.

Following a few days in the hospital, I was transported to a nursing home via a medical ambulance for healing, physical therapy, and ongoing radiation treatments. It was the most challenging and disheartening experience of my life. Nearly two months of confinement in a nursing home, enduring excruciating abdominal pain and being unable to walk, was a formidable trial. To add to my woes, it appeared that the night nurse was pilfering my medication, falsely recording that I had received pain relief when I had not. She was eventually relieved of her duties.

My recovery did not culminate in a finite end at that point; instead, it was a daily journey. The lingering neuropathy in my left leg, at times, causes it to falter during lengthier walks and serves as a gentle reminder of my previous diagnosis. Nevertheless, my gratitude for the mere ability to walk remains profound. It's a detail I sometimes forget until I stumble while walking.

Still, I experienced gradual healing with each passing day, particularly spiritually. It is surprising how much I needed to mend in this area, a realization that only truly struck me after receiving the diagnosis. My faith has grown stronger, and I have come to understand that, eventually, we all must face our mortality. But I do not want to meet that fate without seeking God's face for forgiveness and restoration of my soul. It's a profound journey of healing that encompasses both the body and the spirit.

I must confess that right after the diagnosis, despite my strong faith, I did experience some profound lows. I never questioned God with a "Why me?" but I found myself questioning my faith and relationship with God. It was as if my spirit had been deeply shaken to its core. In the aftermath of the diagnosis, I embarked on a reflective journey through my life. I scrutinized all my actions, searching for any justification for such a fate. I was on a quest to unearth any slip-ups, poor choices, or moments of unworthiness that could explain why I had been singled out to face the challenge of cancer. I found myself asking, *What did I do wrong?* I had this irrational belief that

I must have somehow brought the diagnosis upon myself. Looking back, it is quite ridiculous now, but it was a severe thought of those moments.

Thankfully, this period of doubt and questioning was brief, and I was able to shift my mindset, seeking solace in my faith. I reached out to people in my life who had a strong relationship with God and asked them to pray for me and pray with me. Each person I called upon willingly and earnestly petitioned God on my behalf. In my requests, I made it clear that I did not want them to pray for God to "save" me. Instead, I asked them to pray for God's protection and guidance for my spirit, aligning with whatever plan he had for my life, just as Jesus did in the Garden of Gethsemane, *"Not my but your will be done,"* even if that meant facing mortality. I wanted to be able to accept his will for my life. I had no desire to pray for anything other than what God intended, and I hoped others would not pray for his will to be different from his true desire for me. It was a profound shift in perspective that brought me both comfort and a deep sense of trust.

Once I fully embraced that God was in control and that this experience was something I had to undergo, I set my mind and actions on a new course. In a profoundly humbling act, I prostrated myself before God. I would lay flat on the floor, face down, weep until I could weep no more, and fervently repeat, *"Forgive me. Cleanse me. Make me whole again."* As I uttered these words, I felt the weight of my burden lifted, and I experienced a profound renewal. I would rise from the floor with a lighter heart and a newfound resolve.

I also started placing Psalm 23 in various parts of my daily life. It became a sort of sanctuary. I posted it in my closet, on my bathroom mirror, and even in my tote bags. I recited it every morning, throughout the day, and at night before drifting off to sleep. I firmly held onto the belief that I was walking through the valley of the shadow of death, but I was not alone. God was with me, guiding me. I was resolute in my faith, and even if I faced mortality, I would face it with my faith intact. Even now, nearly two decades after my diagnosis, I occasionally stumble upon postings of Psalm 23 in coat pockets, purses, and various corners of my house. It reminds me of my journey and the unwavering faith that has carried me through.

Other than my faith in God and constant clinging to his promises and grace, I had the affection and love of everyone in my life that helped me stay grounded. My oldest brother, who is now deceased, stood by my side despite his own personal needs and struggles. At that time, I had over two hundred employees; and to my surprise, most of them sent cards, made calls, and even visited me. Strangely enough, they all rallied together to ensure the smooth running of the business during my absence. In their unique way, my girlfriends engaged in friendly squabbles over who was my best friend first (BFF). I look back at it with a laugh now, but I believe they were trying to express how important I was to them and their genuine concern for my well-being. While both of my parents have since passed away, my mother's sister from Chicago (Essie B) came to stay with me, and other aunts and uncles from out of state regularly called and checked in on me. I genuinely felt surrounded by love during my time of illness.

I held on to all the flowers sent to me for years, and my husband humorously dubbed the room where I kept them The Morgue. They were beautifully displayed on a long table in my sunroom, constantly reminding me of the love and support I received during the most challenging period of my life. I eventually decided to part with them after I received the news of being in remission from my doctor five years free from cancer.

The five-second prayer is something that I have held on to longer than I held on to those flowers throughout this cancer journey. My parents had always emphasized the importance of prayer, and I had grown up understanding its significance. The roots of this five-second prayer go back to my teenage years when I was just fifteen years old and found myself contemplating suicide. The reasons were trivial and part of the tumultuous teenage drama that loses its meaning with time. It was a time when I felt constrained by parental expectations and extreme peer pressure.

In my neighborhood, a local church hosted summer Gospel concerts in its parking lot every year. One particular summer, I decided to attend one of these events as a sort of final act before I made the drastic decision to end my life. As I stood on the periphery of the parking lot, a local pastor, known to everyone in the neighborhood, approached me. He was a White man who had moved to our predominantly Black community from Chicago (Rev. Art Erickson).

He asked me, "Can I pray with you?"

Reluctantly and with a tinge of embarrassment, I replied, "Yeah."

I had expected a lengthy prayer, but he finished within seconds to my surprise. I inquired, "Is that it?"

"God already knows what you need. You don't have to spend much time telling him," he responded.

From that moment on, I began saying my own five-second prayer: "forgive me" (as he already knew what I sought forgiveness for), "cleanse me" (with the understanding that he knows what needed cleansing from my mind, body, and spirit), and "make me whole again" (knowing that I had once been whole, but my sins had created a hole that needed repair in my life). It was a profound shift in my prayer practice that focused on the essentials and the belief that God already knows our deepest needs.

The five-second prayer has remained a constant companion in my life since I was fifteen years old. I recite it so frequently daily that it has become as natural as breathing air. The five-second prayer is more than just a security blanket; it's a profound reassurance. It serves as a reminder that life can be unpredictable and end at any moment. By uttering this prayer regularly, I feel that I have taken the time to ask God for forgiveness and prepared my soul for whatever judgment and rest may await in the future.

The ability to pray is a privilege I hold dear and do not take lightly. It is the opportunity for direct communication with God, a gift available to everyone. Believing in God's ever-present care and concern is a matter of personal faith. Knowing that I, or my soul, am never alone or forgotten is one of the most rewarding gifts I've received. This sense of assurance and gratitude is something I acknowledge and share with others.

My parents taught me a valuable lesson—that people do not owe you kindness or favors, so it is a gift to be grateful for when someone does something kind for you. In the same vein, God blessed me and the entire world with the gift of his Son, Jesus Christ. I am forever grateful for this divine act of grace because, in my sin-filled life, God saw value. As a result, I strive to live my life to the fullest every day, embracing the practice of prayer as often as possible.

Even though I have always considered myself rather conservative by nature—despite attending a Baptist church where fervor and exuberance often fill the air and people cry out, run around, and shout—I have sometimes silently thought, *It does not take all of that,* when witnessing such displays of emotion in church.

However, after my diagnosis, I came to understand why some people express their faith in such exuberant ways, especially when they've experienced something profoundly challenging or debilitating. It was a lesson I learned firsthand when I stood before my church congregation and asked for their prayers. At that moment, I felt the power of the Holy Spirit enveloping my life, and I too found myself crying and falling in the spirit.

I can't help but chuckle at myself now as God graciously taught me a valuable lesson about praise and worship through my diagnosis. When he brings you through something so significant, you must share the power of his blessings with others. And whatever it takes to convey that message, you should embrace it wholeheartedly.

CHAPTER 2

What Is Prayer?

In the vast expanse of our lives, there are moments when we embark on miraculous journeys, each with its own unique adventure waiting to unfold, whether it is strapping on a scuba tank to explore the mysteries of the ocean's depths, setting out on a thrilling safari to witness the untamed beauty of the wilderness, or taking that daring leap from a plane for a skydiving experience of a lifetime. One common thread ties all these endeavors together: the belief that something empowering will come out of the experience.

Imagine you are diving into the crystal-clear waters of a coral reef, venturing deep into the heart of the African savannah, or perhaps standing on the crag of that airplane door, ready to plunge into the boundless sky. What do you want more than anything at that moment? It is the assurance that you know what you are getting into, have studied the dynamics, understood the benefits, learned what you would do if things do not go as planned, and acknowledged the potential disadvantages. In essence, you want a clear map before you set off on this exhilarating journey and an assurance that a higher power has your soul covered, regardless of the outcome.

Much like these adventures, our life journey is filled with moments of uncertainty, excitement, and sometimes even trepidation. And just like any explorer or adventurer, we too seek guidance and a compass to navigate the uncharted territories of our hearts and minds. We yearn for a tool that helps us understand the dynamics of our existence, the benefits of our actions, and the potential pitfalls we might encounter. No matter how tough the road might seem, humans have the inquisitiveness to embark on challenging journeys.

That tool is prayer. Just as a seasoned scuba diver studies the underwater terrain, a safari-goer learns about the habits of wild creatures, or a skydiver undergoes rigorous training before taking the leap, so too can we prepare ourselves for the journey of life through the art of prayer.

So what's prayer all about? Well, for a fact, it is not a mere utterance of words into the emptiness of the cosmos. Instead, it's like a deep connection to something much bigger than us, the biggest. Think of it as a special journey, like having a private talk with the owner of this universe, expressing our deepest hopes and dreams, even our fears and vulnerabilities. It is like a boat on a vast, open sea of spirituality, with our faith and trust as the currents guiding us. Prayer isn't just quietly asking for things; it's like the steering wheel that directs our souls and entire lives toward an unseen destination.

Britannica defines prayer as human communication with the sacred—be it God, gods, the transcendent realm, or supernatural powers. But to label prayer solely as a form of communication is akin to describing a grand symphony as mere notes on a page. Prayer is a tapestry woven with threads of human history, spirituality, and the very essence of our existence. In reality, prayer is a mosaic of multidimensional practices as old as humanity. It's like a multifaceted gem, each facet reflecting a different aspect of its brilliance. To truly appreciate its significance, we must peel back these layers individually like explorers embarking on a sacred journey.

1. *A Form of Communication with a Higher Power*

Within the fabric of human existence, prayer is like a thread that intertwines our souls into a sacred dialogue that goes beyond mere words. The bridge connects our hearts with a higher power, a celestial dialogue where our deepest hopes, fears, and aspirations are bare. In the Gospel of Matthew, we find the profound truth: *"But when you pray, go into your room, close the door, and pray to your Father, who is unseen"* (Matthew 6:6 NIV). Here, prayer is not a monologue but a conversation with the unseen Creator of the universe.

Imagine for a moment you're speaking with a close friend, and there's a silent understanding, a connection that goes beyond spoken language. In prayer, it's as if your soul is conversing with a divine friend, sharing your innermost thoughts and feelings. It is a sacred communion that brings solace to the weary heart, strength to the feeble spirit, and hope to the troubled soul. In this divine conversation, we discover that the Creator listens to our words and the unspoken cries of our hearts.

2. *A Two-Way Connection*

Prayer, however, is not a one-sided dialogue where we pour out our thoughts and requests without pause. It's a two-way connection, an invitation for divine guidance and wisdom to flow into our lives. Prophet Jeremiah reminds us of this in his words: *"Call to me, and I will answer you and tell you great and unsearchable things you do not know"* (Jeremiah 33:3 NIV).

Think of it as a phone call to heaven. We speak our concerns and aspirations, and God responds, not necessarily in audible words, but in the gentle stirrings of the heart, the subtle nudges of intuition, and the unfolding events of our lives.

i. *Gentle Stirrings of the Heart*

In 1 Kings 19:12 (NIV), there is a story of the prophet Elijah seeking God's guidance. It says, *"After the earthquake came a fire, but the Lord was not in the fire. And after the fire came to a gentle whisper."* This passage illustrates how God communicated with Elijah through a gentle whisper, stirring his heart and providing guidance.

ii. Subtle Nudges of Intuition

In Acts 16:6–7 (NIV), Paul and his companions were on a missionary journey. The passage says, *"Paul and his companions traveled throughout the region of Phrygia and Galatia, having been kept by the Holy Spirit from preaching the word in the province of Asia. When they came to the border of Mysia, they tried to enter Bithynia, but the Spirit of Jesus would not allow them to."* This example shows how the Holy Spirit guided them through subtle nudges, preventing them from going where they shouldn't.

iii. Unfolding Events of Our Lives

The story of Joseph in the book of Genesis (Genesis 37–50) is an excellent example of God's responses through the unfolding events of one's life. Despite facing adversity and being sold into slavery by his brothers, Joseph eventually became a ruler in Egypt and saved his family during a time of famine. God's plan for Joseph's life was revealed through a series of events, even in the face of challenges and setbacks.

To truly experience the richness of prayer, we must express our desires and open our hearts to receive the divine wisdom and guidance offered in return.

3. *The Heart of Prayer*

In the world of prayer, what truly matters is the sincerity in our hearts, not how fancy our words may be. It is not about crafting perfect sentences but baring our souls before the divine presence. The prophet Samuel was reminded when he was sent to anoint a king: "But the Lord said to Samuel, 'Do not consider his appearance or *height, for I have rejected him. The Lord does not look at the things people look at. People look at the outward appearance, but the Lord looks at the heart"* (1 Samuel 16:7 NIV).

This verse echoes the essence of prayer—it's about the authenticity of our intentions, the purity of our hearts, and the depth of our faith. We need not be eloquent or use flowery language. What matters most is the honesty with which we approach the Divine, laying our true selves bare. In this vulnerability, we find the true power of prayer, for it is in our sincerity that we draw closer to God, forging a bond that transcends words and enters the realm of the sacred.

Understanding what prayer means personally is like laying a solid foundation for a building. It is the cornerstone upon which the entire structure of prayer's potential in your life is built. Think of it like charting a course for a ship. A precise and reliable map is essential before the vessel can navigate the open sea. Similarly, comprehending the essence of prayer, what it personally signifies to you, sets the stage for everything else to align. Once you grasp what prayer means in your heart, it becomes more than a routine or a mere collection of words. It transforms into a powerful force capable of guiding you through life's challenges, offering solace in times of sorrow and magnifying your joy during moments of jubilation.

Your personal understanding of prayer is akin to possessing the key to a treasure chest. As you unlock its true meaning, you gain access to the vast riches of spiritual growth, inner peace, and a deeper connection with the Divine. It's not a one-size-fits-all concept; it's a unique journey you embark upon, evolving and deepening as you expand your understanding and experiences.

Consider the experienced scuba diver once again. They don't just plunge into the ocean without understanding the nature of the aquatic realm they're about to explore. They learn about the behavior of marine life, the currents that may pull them, and the importance of conserving the fragile ecosystem. Similarly, safari-goers don't venture into the wilderness without grasping the purpose of their journey—to witness nature in its unadulterated glory and perhaps gain a deeper connection with the world's wild inhabitants. And a skydiver isn't merely seeking the thrill of free fall; they understand the purpose of their parachute, which is to ensure a safe descent back to solid ground.

Likewise, understanding its true nature and purpose is essential in the realm of prayer. Prayer is an active engagement with the Divine, a conscious effort to connect with God and yield its powerful impacts on our lives. Therefore, learning about the various forms of prayer will guide us better to understanding prayer on a personal level and ignite our soul to cherish the impact of prayer on our lives.

1. *Worship and Praise*

    Within the realm of prayer, a particularly radiant strand is worship and praise. This form of prayer transcends our personal needs and desires; it expresses our profound reverence and acknowledgment of the Divine's greatness. The book of Psalms contains a beautiful verse that encapsulates this sentiment: *"O come, let us worship and bow down: let us kneel before the Lord our maker"* (Psalm 95:6 KJV).

    This verse invites us to recognize God as our Creator and to approach him with hearts full of gratitude and adoration. Worship and praise are like a symphony of our souls, where we lift our voices and spirits to exalt the Divine for his magnificence. It's a way for us to connect with the sacred on a level beyond words, where our hearts sing in unison with the universe.

2. *Petition and Supplication*

    Another essential facet of prayer is the act of petition and supplication. This prayer involves presenting our requests, concerns, and needs before the Divine. Philippians 4:6 (KJV) states: *"Be careful for nothing, but in everything by prayer and supplication with thanksgiving let your requests be made known unto God."*

    This verse encourages us to lay our worries and desires before God, knowing he listens and cares. Petition and supplication are like heartfelt conversations with the Divine, where we share our burdens and seek divine intervention and guidance. It's a reminder that we are not alone in our struggles, and the act of seeking assistance through prayer can bring us comfort and peace.

3. *Intercession*

Intercessory prayer introduces the concept of praying on behalf of others. It is a selfless act of lifting up the needs and concerns of friends, family, and even strangers to the Divine. This idea is beautifully expressed in 1 Timothy 2:1 (NIV): *"I exhort therefore, that, first of all, supplications, prayers, intercessions, and giving of thanks, be made for all men."*

Intercession embodies the essence of empathy and compassion. It is a way to extend our care and support to others, knowing that our prayers can provide comfort and healing. When we intercede, we act as intermediaries, bridging the gap between those in need and the divine source of comfort and strength.

These various forms of prayer—whether in worship and praise, petition and supplication, or intercession—serve as tools to deepen our connection with the Divine. They reflect the multifaceted nature of our relationship with God, encompassing moments of adoration, conversation, and selflessness. Each form has its unique beauty and purpose, contributing to the rich tapestry of prayer that enriches our spiritual lives.

Chapter 3

Why Pray?

Ever wondered why prayer matters in the grand scheme of life? If God already knows everything we need and is both all-powerful and all-loving, shouldn't he just provide without us having to ask? This question often nags at our minds, casting a shadow over our faith journey and disconnecting us from our deeper selves and God's divine plan.

Why is prayer a question that seems logical on the surface, rooted in the profound attributes of God? Scripture tells us that God is all-knowing, assuring us that *"nothing in all creation is hidden from God's sight"* (Hebrews 4:13). It also underscores his omnipotence, proclaiming that he *"does as He pleases with the powers of heaven and the peoples of the earth"* (Daniel 4:35). And let's not forget the heartwarming reminder that *"the Lord is good, and His love endures forever"* (Psalm 100:5).

However, it's important to note that the Bible's broader message extends beyond the concept of prayer. Scripture emphasizes that all our essential needs for a meaningful life and godly existence are abundantly available through a loving and all-powerful God, who anticipates our needs even before we voice them. Nevertheless, the Bible does not teach that these blessings are granted automatically as if they were a given right. Jesus himself conveys this message when he says: *"Ask, and it will be given to you; seek, and you will find; knock, and the door will be opened to you"* (Matthew 7:7).

Similarly, *"have faith in God…whatever you ask for in prayer, believe that you have received it, and it will be yours"* (Mark 11:22, 24). *"This kind can come out only by prayer"* (Mark 9:29). *"Get up and pray so that you will not fall into temptation"* (Luke 22:46). *"If you believe, you will receive whatever you ask for in prayer"* (Matthew 21:22). *"They should always pray and not give up"* (Luke 18:1). The plain and simple truth from these passages, and others like them, is that often, the key to unlocking God's promises lies in our unwavering faith and the practice of heartfelt prayer. We can also see it this way: constant prayer draws us so close to God that we become one with him, which leads him to be gracious enough to unlock these things for us. It is essential to understand that God's blessings touch all, as evidenced by his sun rising on both the righteous and the wicked.

In the Christian journey, prayer, like everything else, is ultimately directed toward God's glory, with our well-being following in that order. All that God does and permits, at the highest level, serves to magnify his glory. At the same time, it's essential to recognize that as God's glory shines, humanity reaps the rewards. Our prayers are a means to honor and glorify God and a channel through which we can receive the blessings he bestows. Even though God possesses omniscience and sees the end from the beginning, prayer remains our special privilege—a way to invite our spirit into the radiance of his infinite grace.

While there are many things we can achieve through prayer, there are certain things we can lose by not praying.

For instance, our neglect of prayer potentially impedes the progress of God's kingdom. The Bible makes it clear that, in the end, God's kingdom will triumph over the earthly kingdoms, and his divine plan will unfold. Yet it also teaches us that prayer is essential to this process. Jesus encourages us to pray for God's kingdom to come and his will to be done on earth, as in heaven. He promises that our prayers, made in his name, will be answered and ultimately bring glory to the Father (John 14:13–14).

Throughout the ministry of the apostle Paul, prayer consistently played a vital role in opening doors for effective service and, notably, in securing his release from prison (Ephesians 6:19, Colossians 4:3–4, 2 Thessalonians 3:1–2, Philippians 1:19). The early apostles too devoted themselves to both prayer and sharing the Word (Acts 6:4). James, in his letter, encourages us to follow the example of the faith and fervent prayer of Elijah, emphasizing that the heartfelt prayer of a righteous person accomplishes much (James 5:16–18).

The undeniable message from these and similar passages is that the Almighty Creator has designed his creation to accommodate the pivotal role of prayer in unfolding his divine plan. In this journey of self-help and faith, we discover that our prayers are not mere words into the void but potent tools that align with God's grand design for his kingdom and are for our benefit.

It is essential to be aware of anything and everything that our prayer can potentially do so we can practice it accordingly and wisely. Understanding the why behind prayer is a powerful revelation as it remarkably transforms our spiritual journey and empowers our faith. When we grasp the purpose and significance of prayer, we unlock the potential for a deeper connection with God and a more meaningful faith-based walk.

For example:

1. *Aligning with God's will. Recognizing that prayer is not only about our requests but also about aligning our desires with God's will empowers believers to pray purposefully.* When we pray "your kingdom come, your will be done," as Jesus taught in Matthew 6:10, we acknowledge that God's plans are greater and more significant than our own. This understanding guides our spiritual journey by leading us to seek God's heart and intentions, fostering a deeper intimacy with him.

2. *Participation in God's work.* The Bible reveals that God often works through the prayers of his people. We are not passive observers in God's grand plan but active participants. This knowledge motivates us to pray fervently, knowing that our petitions can influence and impact our lives.

3. *Receiving God's blessings.* While we understand that God knows our needs before we ask, prayer is how we receive many blessings and promises God has in store. This knowledge encourages believers to pray with expectancy, believing God desires to bestow his goodness upon us. It guides our spiritual journey by fostering a sense of hope, trust, and a deeper relationship with the Giver of all good gifts.

4. *Spiritual growth.* Recognizing the role of prayer in our life helps us mature in our faith. Prayer is not just about asking but about seeking and knocking (Matthew 7:7), which implies a continual pursuit of God. As believers engage in this ongoing conversation with the Creator, we grow in understanding him, drawing nearer to him in the process.

Knowing why we pray empowers believers by providing a clear purpose and direction on our spiritual journey. It encourages believers to align their desires with God's will, actively participate in his work, anticipate his blessings, and grow spiritually. Prayer is not a mere ritual but a dynamic channel for deepening our connection with God and making a meaningful impact in the world. When we pray, God's answers bring about change because prayer is not merely a one-sided conversation where we voice our requests and concerns; it's a profound exchange with the Almighty. It's a dialogue where we communicate our thoughts, desires, and struggles and, in return, receive guidance, wisdom, and empowerment.

Proverbs 3:5–6 reminds us to *"trust in the Lord with all your heart and lean not on your own understanding; in all your ways submit to him, and he will make your paths straight."* This is a powerful illustration of how prayer empowers us to trust in God's wisdom over our own, guiding us along the right path.

Similarly, James 1:5 encourages us to ask God for wisdom, assuring us that he gives it generously without finding fault. This emphasizes the empowering aspect of prayer. When we seek God's wisdom through prayer, we tap into a wellspring of divine knowledge that equips us to navigate life's complexities confidently and clearly. This wisdom empowers us to make wise decisions, handle challenges, and lead purposeful lives.

Prayer is the primary source of strength in adversity. Philippians 4:13 states, *"I can do all things through Him who strengthens me."* Through prayer, we access the strength and resilience we need to face life's trials and tribulations. Prayer empowers us to persevere, overcome adversity, and emerge stronger on the other side. It's a source of comfort and empowerment in times of weakness or hardship.

Including these motivations for prayer in our discussion emphasizes how prayer is a means of making requests and a powerful conduit for empowering us by providing divine guidance, wisdom, and strength. This understanding can motivate us to pray more consistently and purposefully on our spiritual journey.

There are several examples in the Bible that serve various purposes of prayer. Let us have a look at various events:

1. *Spiritual connection (example: Daniel's daily prayers, Daniel 6:10):*

   Now, when Daniel learned that the decree had been published, he went home to his upstairs room, where the windows opened toward Jerusalem. Three times a day, he knelt and prayed, giving thanks to his God, just as he had done before.

Prayer is a powerful means to foster a deep spiritual connection with God. In the face of adversity and a decree forbidding prayer to anyone but the king, Daniel continued his daily practice of seeking God's presence. His unwavering commitment to prayer not only exemplified his devotion but also demonstrated the profound connection he had with the Divine.

2. *Gratitude (example: ten lepers healed, Luke 17:11–19):*

Now, on his way to Jerusalem, Jesus traveled along the border between Samaria and Galilee. As he was going into a village, ten men who had leprosy met him. They stood at a distance and called out in a loud voice, "Jesus, Master, have pity on us!" When he saw them, he said, "Go, show yourselves to the priests." And as they went, they were cleansed. One of them, when he saw he was healed, came back, praising God in a loud voice. He threw himself at Jesus' feet and thanked him—and he was a Samaritan. Jesus asked, "Were not all ten cleansed? Where are the other nine? Has no one returned to give praise to God except this foreigner?" Then he said to him, "Rise and go; your faith has made you well."

Gratitude is an essential element of prayer. This story of the ten lepers healed by Jesus underscores this. While all ten were miraculously cured, only one returned to express gratitude. This account emphasizes how prayer can be a medium for expressing thankfulness for God's blessings and grace.

3. *Seeking guidance (example: King Solomon's prayer for wisdom, 1 Kings 3:5–14):*

At Gibeon, the Lord appeared to Solomon during the night in a dream, and God said, "Ask for whatever you want me to give you…So give your servant a discerning heart to govern your people and to distinguish between right and wrong. Who can govern these great people of yours?…And if you obey me and keep my decrees and commands as David, your father did, I will give you a long life."

Prayer is a way to seek divine guidance and wisdom. King Solomon's famous prayer for wisdom when God offered to grant him anything he desired illustrates this. His request for wisdom instead of wealth or power revealed his recognition of the importance of divine guidance in leadership and decision-making.

4. *Comfort and solace (example: Psalms 23):*

The Lord is my shepherd; I lack nothing.
He makes me lie down in green pastures…
Surely, your goodness and love will follow me all the days of my life,

and I will dwell in the house of the Lord forever.

The book of Psalms is a treasure trove of prayers that offer comfort and solace. Psalm 23, often attributed to King David, is a poignant example. These prayers provide solace during trouble, offering reassurance and strengthening one's faith.

5. *Forgiveness (example: King David's prayer of repentance, Psalm 51):*

   Have mercy on me, O God,
   according to your unfailing love;
   according to your great compassion
   blot out my transgressions.
   Wash away all my iniquity
   and cleanse me from my sin…
   Then you will delight in the sacrifices of the righteous, in burnt offerings offered whole.

   Prayer is a vehicle for seeking forgiveness and reconciliation with God. King David's heartfelt prayer of repentance after his sin with Bathsheba, found in Psalm 51, is a prime example of how prayer can lead to forgiveness and spiritual renewal.

6. *Self-reflection (example: parable of the Pharisee and tax collector, Luke 18:9–14):*

   To some who were confident of their own righteousness and looked down on everyone else, Jesus told this parable: "Two men went up to the temple to pray, one a Pharisee and the other a tax collector. The Pharisee stood by himself and prayed: 'God, I thank you that I am not like other people—robbers, evildoers, adulterers—or even like this tax collector. I fast twice a week and give a tenth of all I get.' ...All those who exalt themselves will be humbled, and those who humble themselves will be exalted."

Prayer can prompt self-reflection and humility. In the parable of the Pharisee and the tax collector, the tax collector's prayer for God's mercy, acknowledging his own shortcomings, highlights the role of prayer in fostering humility and self-awareness.

7. *Community and ritual (example: early Christian community, Acts 2:1–4):*

When the day of Pentecost came, they were all together in one place. Suddenly, a sound like the blowing of a violent wind came from heaven and filled the whole house where they were sitting. They saw what seemed to be tongues of fire that separated and came to rest on each of them. All of them were filled with the Holy Spirit and began to speak in other tongues as the Spirit enabled them.

Prayer often serves as a unifying ritual within religious communities. The early Christian community's gathering for prayer, especially on the day of Pentecost, as described in Acts 2:1–4, emphasizes the communal aspect of prayer, where believers come together to seek God's presence and guidance.

8. *Hope and healing (example: woman who touched Jesus's garment, Mark 5:25–34):*

   And a woman was there who had been subject to bleeding for twelve years. She had suffered a great deal under the care of many doctors and had spent all she had, yet instead of getting better; she grew worse…she thought, "If I just touch the hem of His garment, I will be made whole…He said to her, "Daughter, your faith has healed you. Go in peace and be freed from your suffering."

   Prayer can be a source of hope and healing. This story of the woman who touched the hem of Jesus's garment and was healed (Mark 5:25–34) illustrates how faith-fueled prayers can lead to miraculous healing and restoration.

9. *Giving thanks in advance (example: Jesus's prayer before raising Lazarus, John 11:41–42):*

   So they took away the stone. Then Jesus looked up and said, "Father, thank you for hearing me. I knew that you always hear me, but I said this to benefit the people standing here, that they may believe that you sent me."

   Prayer can also involve giving thanks in advance and showing trust in God's power. Before raising Lazarus from the dead, Jesus

offered a prayer of thanksgiving, acknowledging God's ability and demonstrating
faith in the impending miracle.

10. *Fulfillment of needs (example: Paul and Silas in prison, Acts 16:25–26):*

Paul and Silas were praying and singing hymns to God about midnight, and the other prisoners were listening to them. Suddenly, the prison's foundations were shaken by such a violent earthquake. All the prison doors flew open at once, and everyone's chains came loose.

Prayer is often the key to the fulfillment of various needs. The prayer of the
Apostle Paul and Silas in prison (Acts
16:25-26) resulted in their miraculous
release, highlighting how prayer can lead to
divine intervention and resolving pressing
issues.

Understanding these diverse purposes of prayer and their biblical examples enriches our understanding and appreciation of why we
must pray and the depth and significance of prayer in our spiritual
journey, making it a versatile tool for connection, gratitude, guidance, comfort, and more.

Whom to Pray For?

In the hustle and bustle of our daily lives, it's easy to lose sight of the person at the center of it all—*us*. We often find ourselves immersed in prayers, seeking solutions for external challenges in our professional endeavors or personal relationships. Yet, in the midst of these petitions, we may unintentionally neglect the most vital prayer of all—the one directed inward.

When was the last time you pressed pause, embraced a moment of solitude, and offered up a prayer that harmonized with the cadence of your spirit? I am not implying a plea for your external circumstances, which include your family, friends, work, or social circle, but a sacred whisper for the very core of your being. Perhaps something like, *"Lord, grant me the strength to forgive myself also as I forgive others, the courage to let go,"* or maybe, *"Help me to not lean on my own understanding. Keep me from following my heart because it is deceitful."*

I hear you. It is a bit unconventional to ask, considering our usual prayers are wrapped up in the world around us—family, work, and the whole nine yards. Yet we might miss a subtle truth: in the fervor of praying for others, we sometimes forget to send a few whispers upstairs for ourselves. It is not about sidelining those supplications for others; it is more like realizing an empty pitcher can't fill anyone's cup. Therefore, it is of utmost importance to prioritize self-prayer.

Let's take a moment to reflect on the story of the woman with the issue of blood (Mark 5:25–34). In the midst of a bustling crowd, she sought healing from Jesus by taking the initiative for herself. What's intriguing is her internal dialogue—her belief that if she could touch the hem of his garment, she would be healed. Her story emphasizes the profound connection between internal prayer for herself and outward expression. She did not need grand gestures or loud proclamations; her silent, internal conviction led her to act firmly on her faith. In a way, she engaged in a form of self-prayer—connecting with the Divine within her own heart. This incident also highlights that when we take the initiative to pray for ourselves, God knows the difference and responds to it, just as Jesus did when the woman touched the hem of his garment. He said, *"Someone touched me; I know that power has gone out from me"* (Luke 8:46).

This incident teaches us that the essence of faith often lies in the quiet moments of internal conviction gained through prayer. Like the woman with the issue of blood, our beliefs can drive us to seek a deeper connection with the Divine through personal, heartfelt prayers. It is a reminder that, just as her prayer and faith made her whole again, our internal connection with the Divine through self-prayer can be a source of profound spiritual healing.

It is inevitable that the adversary may try to deceive us, whispering subtle notions about selfishness and moral missteps. A temptation suggests that attending to our spiritual well-being is self-centered, with the adversary asserting, *"You are being selfish by putting yourselves above others."* We must understand that achieving balance in self-prayer is like skillfully managing two plates on a scale—initially demanding conscious effort but evolving into an innate ability with practice, maintaining equilibrium effortlessly. It is critical to realize that neglecting self-prayers leaves us vulnerable to personal struggle and warfare, especially when unequipped to fend off the devil's efforts. The adversary's whispers may gain potency when we lack the fortified strength derived from a consistent practice of self-directed prayer. Recognizing this delicate balance becomes not only a shield against the enemy's wiles but also a source of strength, allowing us to navigate the spiritual battlefield with resilience and confidence. In the faith journey, self-prayer emerges as a vital cornerstone for our spiritual fortitude and steadfastness in Christ.

In Romans 10:10, the apostle Paul imparts a powerful insight: *"For it is with your heart that you believe and are justified, and it is with your mouth that you profess your faith and are saved."* This verse echoes a profound truth—Christian life is a journey that originates within, underscoring the significance of personal prayer. It aligns with the core principles of Christian existence, where prayer and individual communion with Christ stand as foundational pillars. The profession of faith then becomes the focal point of belief and justification. It is a superficial acknowledgment and a profound internal alignment with heart and soul. This inner conviction becomes the push for salvation—an intimate dialogue between the spirit and the Divine.

Similarly, in the context of prioritizing self-prayer, Romans 10:10 illuminates the intrinsic connection between the heart's belief and the spoken profession of faith. The process initiates within the sanctuary of our own spirit, unfolding through intentional moments of oneness with the Divine. As we prioritize self-prayer, we are nurturing the core of our belief, laying the groundwork for a faith that speaks through words and resonates authentically from the depths of our being. It is a journey that highlights the significance of internal transformation, recognizing that the Christian life, at its core, is a profoundly personal and introspective pilgrimage. By prioritizing self-prayer, we embark on a path that aligns our hearts with the Divine, professing a faith that is not just spoken, felt, and experienced but lived every day.

A transformative process unfolds when we genuinely dive into self-prayer to fortify our connection with the Divine. This aligns with Jesus's words from the Gospel of John: *"I am the true vine, and my Father is the vinedresser. Every branch in me that does not bear fruit he takes away, and every branch that does bear fruit he prunes that it may bear more fruit."* As we anchor ourselves in God through his Word and prayer, he molds and purifies us, empowering us to lead a godly life that bears fruit. This spiritual grooming not only helps us resist negative influences but also enables us to intercede for others better and bear witness to the wonders of his grace.

Hence, as we delve into the realm of self-prayer, let our understanding of this balance grow. We must recognize that nurturing our spiritual self is not selfishness but a necessary foundation for leading an exemplary Christian life. In embracing this equilibrium, we contribute to greater spiritual harmony, fostering a profound connection between self-care and communal well-being.

Easier said than done, right? I understand that there exists a common tendency among us to readily lift the needs and concerns of others in intercessory prayer. Yet a noticeable struggle emerges regarding self-pray, particularly outside the context of crises. It is easier for us to run to the altar to fall on our knees and lift our hands and eyes to the Lord. Is a personal prayer on a daily basis too much to do? Is it a mundane concept? Apparently, yes, it is to many of us, but the truth is that this inclination is deeply rooted in various aspects of human nature and incorrect perceptions of God's Word. Interestingly, the Bible provides insights that shed light on this dynamic and show us the right way to pay attention to both responsibilities equally:

1. *External focus in intercessory prayer:*

    In Galatians 6:2, the apostle Paul writes, *"Bear one another's burdens, and so fulfill the law of Christ."* This verse encapsulates a fundamental principle of Christian living—embracing a communal and empathetic approach to the challenges faced by fellow believers. Not just in this letter but throughout the New Testament, we are encouraged not to be solely preoccupied with our individual concerns but to share in the burdens of others actively.

    When we extend our prayers outward, focusing on the needs and challenges faced by those around us, we embody the essence of this biblical encouragement that gives us a sense of achievement since intercessory prayer becomes a tangible expression of bearing one another's burdens, creating a sense of community and fostering empathy within the body of believers.

2. *Reluctance in self-prayer and misplaced humility:*

Conversely, when the time comes for us to engage in self-prayer, a collective hesitancy may linger within our hearts and minds. This hesitancy could arise from a genuine desire to embody humility, a beautiful virtue deeply rooted in the Christian tradition. In our communal understanding, there might be a prevailing notion that it is more virtuous to channel our prayers toward the needs of others rather than to bring our own concerns before God. But we must not fall into this misconception because Satan has this tendency to manipulate us through the Word of God, and he deceives us into the misjudgment that praying for oneself is an act of pride or a lack of humility. The Bible reassures us to approach God confidently with our requests: *"Let us then approach God's throne of grace with confidence, so that we may receive mercy and find grace to help us in our time of need"* (Hebrews 4:16).

Therefore, let us turn our hearts toward the reassurance offered in 1 Peter 5:7, a divine invitation that beckons each of us: *"Cast all your anxiety on him because he cares for you."* In embracing this communal understanding, we recognize that God's caring embrace extends to the collective body of believers and each individual soul within the community.

In these moments of self-prayer, we are reminded that our individual needs and anxieties matter to God. It is not an act of selfishness or a lack of humility to approach the Creator with our personal struggles. Instead, it is an acknowledgment that, just as we fervently intercede for the well-being of others, our own well-being is equally significant in the eyes of our compassionate and caring God.

3. *Crisis-centric self-prayer:*

In self-prayer, we often feel a strong pull toward God during tough times, seeking comfort and guidance instinctively. The Psalms, especially those written by David, capture this sentiment. In Psalm 34, David says, "*This poor man cried, and the Lord heard him and saved him out of all his troubles,*" showing the deep connection formed in moments of need.

Yet self-prayer isn't just for hard times. Psalm 105:4 encourages us to seek God continually, not just when things get tough. It says, "*Look to the Lord and his strength; seek his face always.*" This timeless wisdom reminds us to remember God in struggles and moments of joy, success, and everyday life. By making self-prayer a part of our daily routine, we build a consistent and lively connection with the Divine, enhancing the spiritual journey that leads us to live a godly life, strong in faith and action.

Paul profoundly understood the importance of praying for oneself and others; hence, when he detailed the armor of

God to fight against the devil's schemes, he concluded by saying, *"And* pray *in the Spirit on* all occasions *with* all kinds of prayers and requests. *With this in mind,* be alert *and* always *pray for* all the Lord's people."

4. *Uncomfortable introspection:*

Engaging in self-prayer demands introspection that may feel uncomfortable for some of us. However, the Bible encourages this self-reflection process, as found in Psalm 139:23–24. In these verses, the psalmist humbly implores, *"Search us, God, and know our hearts; test us and know our anxious thoughts. See if there is any offensive way in us and lead us in the way everlasting."*

This heartfelt plea captures the essence of a vulnerable and sincere approach to self-prayer. We seek self-awareness and a transformative journey by inviting God to scrutinize our beings' depths. The request to be tested reflects a profound trust in God's discernment and an earnest desire to align with the righteous path. Thus, Psalm 139:23–24 is an inspirational guide for us to self-pray, encouraging a humble and open-hearted embrace of self-reflection for spiritual growth and alignment with the enduring way that leads to righteousness.

In embracing these dynamics of prayer, let us anchor ourselves in the wisdom that a complete prayer life is a harmonious interplay between intercession for others and personal communion with the Divine. The Bible, as our guiding light, underscores the unity of these facets, urging believers to bear the burdens of those around us and entrust our own needs to a compassionate and attentive God. This integrated approach to prayer is more than a ritual; it is a pathway to a profound connection with the Divine, enriching our spiritual journey. As we navigate the ups and downs of life's challenges and triumphs, may our prayers be a heartfelt dialogue that uplifts the community and nurtures the individual soul, contributing to a flourishing tapestry of faith and well-being.

Chapter 5

Where to Pray?

In exploring the question of where to pray, our minds often direct us to the familiar words of Jesus in the Gospel of Matthew, where he encourages his followers, saying, *"But when you pray, go into your room, close the door and pray to your Father, who is unseen"* (Matthew 6:6). This directive might leave us pondering: *Is the solitary closet the exclusive space for prayer, or does Jesus's teaching usher in a new understanding of where we commune with the Divine?*

As we journey through the Old Testament, we witness a mosaic of prayer unfolding in diverse locations—from altars and high places to tents, synagogues, mountains, and private spaces. Abraham built altars in different landscapes (Genesis 12:7, Genesis 13:18), Moses communed with God in a tent (Exodus 33:7–11), and Daniel found his place of prayer in his home (Daniel 6:10). The spiritual fabric of the Old Testament is woven with instances of heartfelt connection with the Divine, occurring in a variety of settings.

Yet, with Jesus ushering in a new covenant, completing the law, and offering fresh teachings in the "Sermon on the Mount," does his instruction to pray in solitude signal a shift in the where of prayer? Much like how he distilled the multitude of Jewish laws into two fundamental commands (Matthew 22:34–40), is there a new dimension to the act of praying that Jesus is revealing?

In this chapter, we embark on a journey to unravel the layers of this question, seeking a practical understanding and a profound spiritual insight into where and how we commune with our Creator. As we explore the answer to this question, may we discern the time-less wisdom encapsulated in the teachings of Jesus and discover the sacred spaces where our souls can earnestly and authentically connect with the divine presence.

When Jesus instructs us to pray in the seclusion of our rooms, his emphasis lies not in the physical space but in the spiritual disposition of our hearts. This counsel is given in response to a prevalent practice among the Pharisees in those times, who were known to pray showily on street corners, seeking public recognition for their piety. Their prayers became performances staged for the applause of onlookers rather than authentic expressions of genuine communion with the Divine.

Understanding the human tendency toward hypocrisy, where actions may be tailored for public approval while the heart remains distant from sincerity, Jesus redirects our focus. He underscores the importance of an internal, heart-to-heart connection with God over the external display of religious acts. The call to pray in private, behind closed doors, arises from a desire to shield our conversations with the Divine from the pitfalls of seeking approval from the watching eyes of others. Remember, it is not about the place of prayer but intention and priority.

Therefore, Jesus extends an invitation for us to withdraw to the solitude of our rooms, creating a space where authenticity can truly flourish. Much like the common notion that we tend to be more cautious with our words when aware of being observed, this call to private prayer aligns with the idea that genuine expressions thrive in an environment free from external scrutiny.

Reflecting on this, I am reminded of a valuable piece of advice I once came across: "When engaging in an argument, speak as if you are being recorded. This prevents saying things in the heat of the moment that one may later regret." Similarly, in the realm of personal prayer, a sacred avenue to pour out our true selves before our

Heavenly Father, the efficacy of this communion is compromised if we approach it with carefully measured words.

God desires us to approach him as we are, unfiltered and unguarded, trusting that he can transform us into the individuals he envisions. The essence lies in the genuine and open-hearted dialogue that forms the foundation of a close, one-on-one relationship with God through prayer. Through this authentic exchange, we bring our true selves, no matter how raw or unpleasant, that the transformative power of prayer unfolds. In the vulnerability of honest expression, we create a sacred space for God's transformative work to shape us into individuals aligned with his divine purpose.

Regrettably, many individuals find it challenging to embrace the practice of solitude. In a society that often prioritizes individualism, feelings of isolation and loneliness can intensify, causing discomfort when confronted with Jesus's call to solitude. Some may grapple with a sense of despair, questioning if they must endure additional loneliness to connect with God. However, it is crucial to discern that solitude and loneliness are distinct experiences. Solitude represents a healthy form of individualism, fostering personal growth, while loneliness, on the other hand, embodies an unhealthy isolation.

Living in a culture that stresses individual autonomy, balancing solitude and social connection is essential for a thriving Christian life. This equilibrium allows us to be ourselves authentically and fosters meaningful relationships. As Dietrich Bonhoeffer wisely cautions, *"Let him who cannot be alone beware of community…Let him, who is not in the community, beware of being alone…Each by itself has profound perils and pitfalls. One who wants fellowship without solitude plunges into the void of words and feelings, and the one who seeks solitude without fellowship perishes in the abyss of vanity, self-infatuation, and despair."* This guidance emphasizes the importance of navigating the tension between solitude and sociality to cultivate a wholesome spiritual and relational existence.

In the New Testament, we come across profound instances of Jesus and his apostles immersing themselves in prayer, emphasizing the significance of solitude on their spiritual journey. These examples not only highlight but illuminate the crucial role of retreating to solitary places for the purpose of connecting with the Divine with authenticity. One notable instance is Jesus's prayer in the Garden of Gethsemane (Matthew 26:36–46). Faced with the impending crucifixion, Jesus retreated to this quiet garden, and even though Jesus took three of his apostles, Peter, James, and John, with him, he asked them to wait at a distance so he could have some time alone with his Father in heaven, pouring out unfiltered requests and showing God his vulnerable self: *"Father, if you are willing, take this cup from me; yet not my will, but yours be done"* (Luke 22:42). It serves as a poignant reminder that in moments of profound significance, finding a quiet place away from the distractions of the world allows for a focused and undisturbed conversation with God.

The Mount of Olives is another significant location where Jesus sought solitude for prayer (Luke 22:39–46). Away from the crowds and in the stillness of the night, Jesus engaged in heartfelt communication with the Father. This exemplifies the intentional choice of a crowd-free environment, emphasizing the value of a quiet, undisturbed space.

Turning to the apostles, the example of Peter praying on the rooftop offers a unique insight (Acts 10:9–23). In this instance, Peter's solitude on the rooftop becomes a backdrop for a transformative vision. The act of seeking isolation allowed him to focus solely on God, emptying himself from worldly distractions. This illustrates an essential aspect of solitary prayer—by removing ourselves from the noise and clamor of the world, we create space for God's work to take place within us, preparing us for the challenges and revelations that may lie ahead. We, like Peter, open up a spiritual sanctuary for God's transformative work. In the stillness of that rooftop prayer, Peter was being prepared for a momentous encounter—a visit to Centurion Cornelius. The act of seeking solitude was not merely a withdrawal from the world; instead, it was a way to let God reveal his will and plan to him and initiate a preparation.

These examples emphasize that solitary prayer is not a retreat from reality but a conscious decision to carve out a hallowed haven where diversions diminish, creating an opportunity for a profound connection with the Divine. In these uninterrupted moments of connection, we open ourselves to the profound influence of God's craftsmanship, preparing our hearts for the path he has mapped out for us.

We are pretty much sorted now that to foster a deep connection with God through prayer and undivided attention, solitary places are where we ought to retreat. In the sacred realm of prayer, the notion of solitude has transcended the physical constraints of rooms or closets. It brings us to the realization that the Lord, our God, is omnipresent, a divine reality beautifully articulated in Psalm 139:7–10. *"Where can I go from your Spirit? Where can I flee from your presence? If I go up to the heavens, you are there; if I make my bed in the depths, you are there. If I rise on the wings of the dawn, if I settle on the far side of the sea, even there, your hand will guide me; your right hand will hold me fast."*

Here, we are reminded that there is no corner of existence where God's Spirit is absent. God is there whether we ascend to the heavens or make our abode in the depths. Even if we take the wings of the morning and dwell in the uttermost parts of the sea, his guiding hand is ever-present, and his right hand securely holds us. This omnipresence takes on even more profound significance in the aftermath of Jesus's sacrificial act on the cross. The tearing of the temple curtain that once separated the holy from the most holy speaks volumes. It echoes the fulfillment of Jesus's words to the Samaritan woman, heralding a new era of prayer and worship. No longer confined to specific mountains or cities, true worshippers are invited to commune with the Father in the Spirit and in truth.

Let us imagine the divine curtain, torn from top to bottom, granting unrestricted access to the presence of God. It is a revolutionary shift, an invitation to worship not bound by physical locations but anchored in the Spirit and in truth.

Now, amid our exploration of prayer, let us shift our attention to our short yet all-encompassing prayer, *"Forgive me. Cleanse me. Make me whole again. Amen."* This five-second prayer, simple yet profound, wraps within it a call for forgiveness, purification, and restoration. What sets this prayer apart is its adaptability and versatility.

1. *Anywhere, anytime.* It is not confined to specific spaces like rooms or closets. In fact, it is a prayer for every moment, a sacred utterance that fits anywhere, anytime. As you have seen in your spiritual journey, God's presence is not limited; it is with you wherever you are, as emphasized in Matthew 18:20, *"For where two or three gather in my name, there am I with them."*

   So, whether you are navigating the hustle of the day or finding solace in the quiet of the night, this five-second prayer unfolds as a complete offering—a chance to seek forgiveness, cleansing, and the restoration of wholeness. It serves as your swift connection to the Divine, a whisper echoing an entire conversation with the Creator. Consider this prayer an ever-present companion, a brief yet profound way to commune with the One who is always there, listening, and ready to extend his grace and mercy. Amen.

2. *Morning and night.* As the sun graces the sky with its first light, embrace the opportunity to align your spirit with divine grace through the five-second prayer. In the morning, let the words *"Forgive me. Cleanse me. Make me whole again. Amen."* Set a positive tone for the day ahead. As you offer your requests to the Lord, remember the assurance in Psalm 5:3, *"In the morning, Lord, you hear my voice; in the morning, I lay my requests before you and wait expectantly."*

   Similarly, in the quiet moments before you lay down to rest, allow the five-second prayer to be a gentle conclusion to your day. Seek forgiveness, cleansing, and the restoration of wholeness, trusting in the continuous guidance of the God of your life. *"By day the Lord directs his love, at night his song is with me—a prayer to the God of my life"* (Psalm 42:8).

3. *Before work or school.* Before embarking on the day's endeavors, let the five-second prayer become a source of strength and guidance, especially as you head to work or school. In those moments, offer the words *"Forgive me. Cleanse me. Make me whole again. Amen"* as a sincere plea for God's guidance. Recognize that through this prayer, you seek personal forgiveness, cleansing, and the strength to live a righteous life.

As you step into your workplace or educational environment, carry with you the assurance that you have been forgiven and cleansed. Let this confidence in God's grace empower you to set an example as a follower of God wherever you go. In praying these words, you align your intentions with a desire for righteousness, aiming to be a living testament to the transformative power of God's forgiveness and cleansing and making you whole again.

4. *During emotional states.* Whether in moments of joy, sorrow, motivation, or discouragement—the five-second prayer emerges as a steadfast companion. As we navigate the spectrum of our feelings, consider offering the simple yet profound words, *"Forgive me. Cleanse me. Make me whole again. Amen."* This prayer is not confined to specific emotions but is a versatile expression that transcends the highs and lows of our inner world.

   Drawing inspiration from Philippians 4:6–7, we are reminded, *"Do not be anxious about anything, but in every situation, by prayer and petition, with thanksgiving, present your requests to God. And the peace of God, which transcends all understanding, will guard your hearts and minds in Christ Jesus."*

   Let this prayer be a humble acknowledgment of gratitude in moments of happiness. In times of sadness, let it be a plea for comfort. When motivation surges, let it be a prayer for guidance. And in the face of discouragement, let it be a resilient declaration of reliance on God's transformative power. In every emotional state, the five-second prayer becomes a source of solace, joy, and resilience—an anchor tied to the unchanging presence of the Divine.

5. *In idle moments.* In those quiet intervals scattered throughout the day—moments caught between the hustle and bustle, during daydreams, or while waiting in line—seize the opportunity to utter the five-second prayer. As your mind may wander into temptations or ungodly thoughts, let these idle moments become a sanctuary for a quick prayer. Offer the words *"Forgive me. Cleanse me. Make me whole again. Amen"* as a shield against distractions, a compass for guidance, and a source of inner peace.

These seemingly insignificant pauses transform idle time into sacred moments connecting with the Divine.

6. *Embrace frequent prayer.* Encouraged by the wisdom of 1 Thessalonians 5:17, which invites us to *"pray continually,"* find comfort in the notion that praying often is not only acceptable but truly encouraged. Emphasize the simplicity of the five-second prayer, making it easy to repeat throughout the day. Let this brief yet meaningful prayer become a regular part of your daily rhythm, creating a consistent thread of connection with the Divine. Whether in the midst of busyness or in moments of quiet reflection, allow the repetition of the five-second prayer to be a gentle reminder of the ongoing intimacy with the Divine that is both accessible and inviting.

7. *Prayer as a lifestyle.* Envision prayer not as an occasional guest but as an engaging companion in your daily life. Seamlessly integrate the five-second prayer into your routine, transforming it from a mere task into a vibrant lifestyle aspect. Picture this prayer as a trusted friend walking alongside you on the dynamic journey of life.

   Encourage yourself and fellow travelers on this spiritual path to make the five-second prayer a constant presence—a comforting melody that accompanies every step. Embrace the joy of experiencing God's presence in ordinary and extraordinary moments of life. While it might initially seem challenging, remember that shaping a lifestyle requires conscious and continuous effort. Start with the five-second prayer, let it become a familiar rhythm, and witness how this simple practice adds vibrancy and depth to your daily experience.

As we wrap up our thoughts on where to pray, let us take a moment to appreciate the delicate balance between the sacred and the everyday. It is not about pinpointing specific spots or sticking to a strict schedule; it is more like inviting prayer to be part of our whole lives. The five-second prayer, a simple yet powerful way to connect, has become a flexible companion in our spiritual journey. It is not just a set of words; it is like chatting with the Divine that goes beyond time and place. Whether facing the challenges of the day, riding the waves of our emotions, or finding quiet moments in between, we have realized that prayer is not confined to specific times or spots.

It is a kind of ever-present energy that nudges us to the divine melody playing in the background of our lives. As we integrate prayer into the very fabric of who we are, it shifts from occasional practice to a steady part of our daily talk with the Creator. It is a continuous connection that does not ask for grand gestures but thrives in the simplicity of being real.

So, as we finish up this chapter, let us carry the heart of prayer wherever we go. Let it be like a familiar tune, a comforting presence, and a constant reminder that we are in touch with the Divine in ordinary and extraordinary times. This prayer journey is not a straight road with a set destination; it is more like a sacred rhythm blending with our hearts' beats and our souls' whispers.

Chapter 6

How to Pray?

Imagine you are gearing up for a holiday or special dinner celebration at your home—a joyous occasion calling for meticulous planning and thoughtful execution. Your goal: to host a buffet that leaves everyone satisfied and smiling. Now think of prayer in a similar light—a purposeful activity that requires preparation and a clear understanding of how to achieve its intended outcome.

Crafting meaningful prayers, much like planning a buffet, requires some thoughtful preparation. I am not referring to spontaneous prayers that emerge in moments of joy or sorrow but rather the intentional, scheduled prayers that are a consistent part of our routine. Just as you might meticulously research new recipes and compile a shopping list for a buffet, effective prayer involves a bit of groundwork. It is about setting aside dedicated time, creating a conducive environment, and approaching the act of prayer with purpose and reflection. You might explore different prayer methods, gather the necessary spiritual "ingredients," and lay them out to ensure a harmonious connection with the Divine. Just as you would not throw all ingredients into the pan, hoping for the best, you would not want to approach prayer haphazardly—especially when aiming to bring out the richness of your spiritual experience. Carefully and systematically adding elements to your prayer routine allows you to achieve the best-desired results, much like the thoughtful preparation required for a successful culinary endeavor.

Interestingly, to get rid of throwing everything and anything into the pot of prayer to make a delicious soul-calming soup, Jesus has given us a great recipe, telling us in Matthew 6:7–31 what not to do, *"And when you pray, do not heap up empty phrases as the Gentiles do, for they think that they will be heard for their many words,"* followed by what to do, as recorded in verses 9 to 13. Yes, that is the "Lord's Prayer."

He discourages a mechanical, repetitive approach, emphasizing that God, our Father, already knows our needs; according to Matthew 6:8, *"Your Father knows what you need before you ask him."* As shown by these teachings, effective prayer transcends a mere list of requests. Instead, it is a deep connection, a spiritual conversation with the Almighty constituted of various important components of the "Lord's Prayer" as guided in Matthew 6:9–13. It starts by acknowledging the holiness of God, setting a tone of reverence and awe, much like carefully choosing decor for a celebration to align with its significance.

The prayer then expresses a desire for God's will to be done on earth as in heaven, emphasizing the surrender of personal desires to a higher purpose—a sentiment similar to understanding the broader goal of a celebration beyond individual preferences. Following this is a request for daily sustenance, akin to planning a buffet considering the needs of your guests. Effective prayer involves recognizing our dependence on God for daily spiritual nourishment.

Forgiveness and seeking protection from temptation and evil conclude the "Lord's Prayer," highlighting the importance of humility, accountability, and spiritual discernment—essential elements in crafting an effective prayer.

If you notice, nothing said in the "Lord's Prayer" is shallow. In fact, everything is purposeful, which makes it a wholesome prayer as it covers all essential aspects of a person's life. Submission to God the Father concerns oneself and then touches on our connection to people. "Lord's Prayer" is not just a ritualistic chant but a constant reminder and surrender to continue obeying Christ's two greatest commandments: "Thou shalt love the Lord thy God with all thy heart, soul, and mind. This is the first and greatest commandment. And the second is like unto it; Thou shalt love thy neighbor as thyself."

I do not mean to suggest that your prayers should be confined solely to the "Lord's Prayer" because each of these components is like vast oceans with a whole world within them, which you discover when you delve into and explore them. Therefore, I aim to emphasize the significance of the pattern and organization we can glean from the "Lord's Prayer" because what could be better than learning from himself?

Effective prayer involves not only speaking your side of the story in a systematic way (which I encourage), but it is also an exploration of our hearts. Jeremiah 17:9–10 tells us that our *heart is deceitful and beyond cure; who can understand it?* Then it continues to say that *the* LORD *searches the heart and examines the mind.* So if God knows about it and we want to know about it too or at least understand its ways so we can work on them and align our desires with the divine purpose, do not you think God is our go-to person for that? And how is that going to happen?

In the Bible story in 1 Samuel 3:10, there's this particular moment when Samuel hears God's voice in the quiet of the night. Samuel, the son of Hannah, a barren woman, was born in response to her prayers at the tabernacle. As a result, she dedicated him to the service of the Lord from a young age.

His story in chapter 3 teaches us something important about prayer—it is like having a two-way talk with God. But here's a thought: *When people like Moses, Samuel, David, or others heard God, do you think it was when they were talking, or were they quiet, letting God speak?* Now think about our prayers. Usually, we say our part and then just get up and go. We do not wait quietly to hear what God might want to say. We forget to let his Spirit guide our thoughts and hearts.

Here is a tip on how to pray. After you have said your part in prayer, take a moment to be still. See if God has something to share. It is not just about talking; it is about listening too. And you know what helps? Reading God's Word and spending quiet time with him. That way, you create a space where God's voice can speak to you and guide you. That is when prayer becomes complete, and the true meaning is fulfilled when we say it is a conversation.

Just as Samuel attentively listened to God's voice, you are encouraged to be willing to listen during your prayer moments. It goes beyond the recitation of words; it beckons you to create a space of quiet receptivity. In the hustle of your lives, you may often bombard God with your words, desires, and concerns, yet the essence of prayer lies in speaking and in allowing moments of silence for God to speak to your heart and calm it.

As we embark on this journey of two-way communication with God, let Samuel's receptive heart serve as a guiding light. Let us willingly set aside quiet time in our prayer moments, creating an atmosphere where we express our thoughts and open our hearts to receive divine guidance, comfort, and revelation. In this harmonious exchange, the true beauty of prayer unfolds—a dialogue where we speak and, more importantly, we listen.

Here are a few practical tips to develop an effective prayer routine:

1. *Find a quiet place.* Effective prayer involves creating a conducive environment. You might want to remove distractions and unnecessary clutter. It is about setting the stage for a purposeful encounter with the Divine. Picture a bustling city with noisy streets, horns blaring, and people rushing that constantly distract you from working or focusing on an important thing. Amid this chaos, imagine a serene park, a hidden oasis of tranquility. Like in the city's hustle, our lives can be noisy and demanding. Finding a quiet place for prayer is like discovering that peaceful park in the midst of chaos. Find a calm and distraction-free

place to pour out your thoughts easily. It is the same way with prayer, which is also why Jesus mentioned praying privately.

Jesus used to find quiet spots, sometimes in the garden, at other times on mountaintops. So do something similar. Set up a simple sanctuary in one corner of a room—no distractions, just a place to connect with God. In this little sacred space, you will find peace and make your prayers feel more personal and closer and, above all, honest and unfiltered.

2. *Set a regular time.* Despite the hustle and bustle, long for a deeper connection with God. Drawing inspiration from Daniel, who was committed to praying three times daily, try to set up a regular prayer routine. Every morning, before the world awakes, or in the evening, as the day settles into stillness, carved out moments for prayer. It is not about rigid schedules; instead, it will become a rhythm, a natural flow woven into the fabric of your day. Through intentional practice, David discovered consistency, making prayer a guiding force throughout his day.

The Bible supports the idea of setting aside regular times for prayer. In Psalm 5:3 (NIV), David says, "In the morning, Lord, you hear my voice; in the morning, I lay my requests before you and wait expectantly." This verse underscores the value of starting the day with prayer, which creates a communion with God. Similarly, in 1 Thessalonians 5:17 (NIV), the apostle Paul encourages believers to "pray continually," emphasizing the importance of an ongoing conversation with God throughout the day.

3. *Prayer posture.* Kneeling, standing, and even walking help to develop a prayer posture, which becomes a tool to connect one's heart with God. At times, you may stand in awe, soaking in the marvel of God's creations, while at other moments, you may kneel down, expressing humility before the Divine. In these instances, the physical becomes a doorway to the spiritual, adding a meaningful layer to your prayer experience.

As we tread further into the realms of effectual prayer, it becomes evident that the posture of our hearts shapes the substance of our communication with the Divine. The practical tips shared earlier, like finding a quiet place, setting a regular time, and considering prayer postures, serve as the foundation for what we are about to experience in our prayer journey. Imagine these tips as the frame of a door, and let us open that door to unveil the essential guidelines for effective prayer. This journey encompasses adoration, confession, thanksgiving, supplication, and intercession.

1. *Adoration and praise.* Embark on your prayer journey by picturing a grand cathedral, its majestic spires reaching toward the heavens. The air is thick with adoration and praise as you enter its entrance. This sets the tone for effective prayer—entering the divine presence with hearts brimming with adoration and praise.

   Consider the example of Hannah, the mother of Prophet Samuel, a woman entrenched in her struggles yet offering a prayer saturated with profound adoration. She did not just bring her requests; she praised God for his sovereignty and grace. Hannah's prayer resonates with the spirit of Psalm 100:4, which encourages entering the gates with thanksgiving and the courts with praise. Hannah teaches us that adoration is not a mere formality but a gateway to intimacy with the Creator. Recall when Paul says, in Hebrews 4:16, *"Let us approach the throne of grace confidently."*

Similarly, think of the Psalms written by David, often beginning with expressions of praise and adoration. For instance, Psalm 103:1–2 (NIV) says, *"Praise the Lord, my soul; all my inmost being, praise his holy name. Praise the Lord, my soul, and forget not all his benefits."* David's psalms underscore the transformative power of beginning prayers with adoration, acknowledging God's character, and expressing gratitude for his goodness.

Moreover, in the New Testament, the "Lord's Prayer" in Matthew 6:9–13 starts with adoration, addressing God as *"Our Father in heaven, hallowed be your name."* Jesus's model prayer emphasizes the importance of recognizing God's holiness and starting our prayers with adoration. So let the grand cathedral of adoration be the entry point for your prayers, drawing inspiration from biblical examples that highlight the transformative impact of praising and adoring God in the beginning stages of your conversation with him.

2. *Confession and repentance.* Envision a tranquil garden where the sweet scent of flowers blends with the gentle rustle of leaves. In this peaceful haven, think of David, weighed down by the burden of his transgressions, earnestly pouring out his heart in repentance. His prayer in Psalm 51 is a moving illustration of confession and repentance.

   Effective prayer entails recognizing our shortcomings and sincerely seeking forgiveness. David's humility and deep regret provide valuable guidance, underscoring that confession is not a display of weakness but a route to spiritual renewal. Much like David discovered solace in repentance, our prayers strengthen when we approach God with transparency and a contrite heart.

   Consider also the words of the apostle John in 1 John 1:9 (NIV): "If we confess our sins, he is faithful and just and will forgive us our sins and purify us from all unrighteousness." This biblical verse reinforces the importance of confession in our prayer life and highlights God's faithfulness in granting forgiveness and cleansing.

Confession and repentance are recurring themes in the Bible, showcasing individuals like the prodigal son (Luke 15:18–21) and the tax collector (Luke 18:13–14) finding reconciliation through humble repentance. These stories echo the truth that admitting our mistakes and seeking God's mercy is a powerful and transformative aspect of effective prayer.

So let the quiet garden of repentance be a place of reflection in your prayers, drawing inspiration from David and others who found spiritual renewal through sincere confession before the Divine.

3. *Thanksgiving.* In Matthew 14:19, the moment Jesus gives thanks serves as a poignant reminder that thanksgiving is a crucial element of effective prayer. It nurtures a spirit of appreciation for God's provisions.

Reflect on the apostle Paul's words in Philippians 4:6 (NIV): *"Do not be anxious about anything, but in every situation, by prayer and petition, with thanksgiving, present your requests to God."* Here, thanksgiving is intertwined with prayer, emphasizing its significance in communicating with God.

The Bible is filled with gratitude, such as the ten lepers healed by Jesus, with only one returning to express thanks (Luke 17:11–19). This story underscores the transformative power of gratitude in our interactions with God.

So let the image of the banquet table be a reminder in your prayers—a reminder to express heartfelt gratitude, follow the example of Jesus, and understand that thanksgiving is a crucial element that enriches our connection with God.

4. *Supplication and intercession.* Imagine a vibrant orchestra where each instrument contributes its unique melody. Similarly, our prayers are a symphony, combining personal requests (supplication) and intercession for others. Consider the apostle Paul as the conductor, fervently praying for the churches, as seen in Ephesians 1:16–18.

Effective prayer transcends personal concerns, extending to the needs of others. Paul's example is a powerful illustration of intercession, demonstrating how our prayers can harmonize into a source of blessing and healing for those around us. James 5:16 emphasizes the impact of fervent prayer: "*Therefore confess your sins to each other and pray for each other so that you may be healed. The prayer of a righteous person is powerful and effective.*" This verse underscores the potency of our prayers, highlighting that sincere and heartfelt intercession can bring about significant positive change in our lives and those we influence. Through supplication and intercession, our prayer life becomes a dynamic symphony, resonating with the powerful chords of positive transformation.

As we wrap up this chapter on how to pray, it is like we are at a crossroads—a place where purpose, practice, and guidance meet. Understanding how to pray is like having a compass, helping our hearts connect with the Divine meaningfully. And the practical tips? They are like special keys, unlocking doors to quiet moments, a routine, and postures that make our time with God really special. But what is the real heart of an effective prayer? It uses those guidelines—adoration, confession, thanksgiving, supplication, and intercession. Think of it like a journey that is totally connected to why we talk to God. It is not a strict rulebook but a mix of understanding, practice, and guidance, creating a beautiful symphony that connects us with the Creator.

So, as we think about all these, let us keep within us the spirit of how to pray effectively. May our prayers be more than words—a real conversation between God and us. Remember, the purpose is like our guiding star, the tips are like our trusty friends, and the guidelines are our compass in this sacred prayer journey.

CHAPTER 7

Forgive Me

Much like a biblical narrative, life today is a mosaic of imperfections and judgments from people around us. Ever since the first sin, humans have been prone to sinning because of its presence in human nature. Woefully, man did not have to reach a certain threshold or count of sin to lose the badge of perfection; all it took was one sin and *boom*.

Even after decades and centuries of that downfall, it's a universal truth, a shared experience that binds us all together and tells us that we all are in the same boat. The letter to Romans 3:23 says, "For all have sinned and fallen short of the glory of God." Hence, it is not suitable for a sinner to judge another sinner for sinning differently. Jesus said, "Let he who is without sin cast the first stone."

We must recognize and acknowledge that we all have our fair share of sins and imperfections, which is the initial key to asking God to *"forgive me"* because we need God's grace that helps us to embrace ourselves fully. It's like looking in the mirror and acknowledging that there are flaws, but that doesn't define our worth. In fact, it opens the door to self-acceptance, an essential journey toward spiritual growth. The fact is that we can only correct a mistake once we realize that it is a mistake. Similarly, until and unless we accept that we are sinners and need forgiveness, we will remain entangled in the web of ignorance, self-pity, and self-blame and continue to repeat the same sins and mistakes because we do not deem them to be actions that keep us from God's grace and from becoming a person after God's heart. Remember that even in these times, it is not the sins that keep us from God's grace. But we refuse to acknowledge that we need restoration because the second letter to Corinthians tells us that God's grace is sufficient for us. His grace can forgive and cover any sin, no matter how big.

It's not really the size of our mistakes that keep us from turning back to God; it's more about not realizing or not wanting to return to God the Father. Sometimes, we get stuck in our wrongdoing and continue to feel guilty about our past mistakes. That's where Satan comes in—he's the king of lies. He loves to remind us of all the bad stuff we've done. Why? Because he wants us to think we're no good and keep us away from God. He knows that when we believe in the forgiveness of Jesus, our sins are all wiped away. But he doesn't want us to know that because then we might turn back to God and be saved. So he tricks us into thinking we're worthless and good for nothing. The key is to see through these lies and remember that God loves us no matter what, and we're forgiven when we believe in the saving power and grace of Jesus Christ.

Hence, we must let go of unrealistic expectations and realize that making mistakes is a natural part of being human—it's in our nature, something we can't handle on our own. If we could, there wouldn't have been a need for Christ's sacrifice. This understanding isn't an excuse to keep making bad choices but an invitation to be kind to ourselves and eventually extend that kindness to others. It's a chance to rely more on God's power, strength, and the Holy Spirit than our efforts and intentions.

Apostle Paul, in pointing out our past shortcomings due to sin, also shows us a better way: "All are justified freely by his grace through the redemption that came by Christ Jesus" (Romans 3:24). He emphasizes the idea of boasting in weaknesses so Christ's power may be at work in us: "I will boast all the more gladly about my weaknesses, so that Christ's power may rest on me" (2 Corinthians 12:9). This highlights the shift from our fallen state to a state of justification through God's grace, encouraging us to find strength not in our perfection but in Christ's power working in our imperfections.

We must not forget that God is kind and merciful, and even though he is throned in heaven of heavens, his heart goes out to his people, and he cares for his very creation. Knowing that humans, burdened by their sinful nature, couldn't justify themselves through their actions alone, God provided this profound solution—his abundant grace and mercy, a gift freely given, not contingent on our performance. Once we accept and ask for forgiveness, this grace by believing in Christ as our Savior, our sins no longer disqualify us from his unmerited favor.

Unlike human relationships that often come with conditions and expectations based on our actions, God's love is unconditional. It's a love that doesn't depend on how much good we do or how well we perform. If it did, Christ's sacrifice for our forgiveness would be unnecessary. Yet, as Paul emphasizes, "But God demonstrates his own love for us in this: While we were still sinners, Christ died for us" (Romans 5:8).

In the same way, God accepts us as we are and then works on making us better. We should extend the same grace to ourselves. It's a gentle reminder not to be too harsh or critical of our own shortcomings. Embracing self-acceptance doesn't mean complacency; it acknowledges our imperfections while recognizing the transformative power of grace in our lives. Just as God's love propels us toward positive change, our self-acceptance catalyzes personal growth. By fostering a compassionate view of ourselves, we open the door to healing and transformation that comes from forgiveness.

When we ask for God's forgiveness, it's not only about asking him for help but acknowledging that we are sinners and are forgiving ourselves. Just like when we apologize to God and ask him to forgive our mistakes, we should also be kind to ourselves. It's like treating our own hearts with the same kindness we ask from God. Consider it like this: Jesus, who did all those fantastic miracles, often said, "Have faith in God. I tell you the truth, you can say to this mountain, may you be lifted up and thrown into the sea, and it will happen." But you must really believe it will happen and have no doubt in your heart.

It's like he's saying our belief is essential for God to work in us. Our faith, or what we truly believe in our hearts, plays a significant role.

So when we're asking for forgiveness, it's not just about saying the words. It's also about believing that God can/has forgiven us and being kind to ourselves in the process. It's like having faith that God's love is big enough to cover our mistakes and help us become better. Just like Jesus said in the Bible, "Your faith has made you well" (Luke 18:42). It's a reminder that our belief in God and ourselves can bring about positive changes in our lives.

Consider this parable of the Pharisee and the tax collector in Luke 18:9–14, which illustrates humility's importance in seeking forgiveness. In this story, the Pharisee, known for his religious devotion, stands proud and self-righteous in the temple, listing his virtues. On the other hand, the tax collector, aware of his shortcomings, stands humbly before God, pleading for mercy. This parable underscores the transformative power of humility in the process of seeking forgiveness. Like the tax collector, acknowledging our imperfections and approaching God with a humble heart opens the door to his mercy. On the other hand, the Pharisee's pride becomes a barrier to genuine repentance and the experience of God's forgiveness.

Therefore, when we seek God's forgiveness, we must also humbly accept our need for his mercy and acknowledge our sins. In doing so, we align our hearts with the Divine, creating space for transformation and allowing his forgiveness to become a holistic and profound experience because harboring pride, self-blame, and guilt, even after seeking God's forgiveness, hinders the whole experience of grace. Therefore, to savor the complete taste of God's grace, we must release our burdens and embrace the freedom that comes with self-forgiveness. In extending this kindness to ourselves, we open our hearts to receiving more goodness from a life spent in Christ.

The simplicity of the five-second prayer ("God, Forgive me. Cleanse me. Make me whole again. Amen.") summarizes a profound process that begins with seeking forgiveness from Almighty God. In uttering these words, we acknowledge our inherent sinfulness, recognizing our deep need for God's boundless mercy and grace. This acknowledgment fills humility within us, teaching us that, no matter how praiseworthy our efforts may be, our inherent imperfection persists, and the journey involves inevitable stumbles.

This humility is crucial for realizing we can't navigate this journey alone. Despite our best intentions, our goodness will always fall short. Yet this understanding isn't an excuse to stay down but an invitation to let God pick us up. The five-second prayer guides us to rise from our moments of weakness and seek restoration in God's unwavering love.

Connecting this humility and seeking of forgiveness to the stories Jesus shared, we find guidance in two parables: that of the self-righteous Pharisee and the humbled tax collector and the tale of the wayward prodigal son who returned to a forgiving father. These stories emphasize the importance of avoiding the pitfalls of self-righteousness or succumbing to the weight of prolonged guilt and shame. Instead, they teach us to embrace humility, seek forgiveness, and trust God's willingness to restore and welcome us back.

Furthermore, as we reflect on our personal journey and seek forgiveness, it becomes evident that our unique alignment with our Savior is paramount. Matthew 7:3–5 highlights the significance of addressing our shortcomings before assisting others, like fixing our eyesight before attempting to help someone else see clearly. This emphasizes the importance of cultivating a solid foundation through a personal relationship with Christ. By doing so, we strengthen our faith and deepen our connection with Christ, ensuring that when we extend help to others, it is rooted in authenticity and a genuine understanding of God's grace. In essence, the five-second prayer becomes a transformative journey—starting with seeking God's forgiveness.

Even after seeking forgiveness and embarking on a journey to live a life reflecting Christ, it's essential to acknowledge that the adversary, Satan, doesn't relent in trying to fail our joy and peace found in Christ. The first thing that prompts after seeking forgiveness is a crucial shift toward change, a desire to transform ourselves. To facilitate this change, spending quality time with God becomes not just a necessity but a foundation-building practice, like gearing up for the challenges that lie ahead.

We must examine our relationships as we decide to change and follow Christ. We should think about the people around us and choose those who support our decision to follow Jesus. It's like making sure our friends and connections match the new way we want to live. Sometimes, distancing ourselves from influences that hinder our growth becomes imperative. However, it's not uncommon for Satan to exploit this moment, tempting us to believe that withholding kindness from specific individuals or breaking ties with them contradicts our Christian journey. Yet this needs to be clarified. Reflecting on Christ's own preparations before ministering to others reminds us that self-care and preparation are integral steps.

The idea that prioritizing our own needs is an act of selfishness is a common misunderstanding. The wisdom lies in recognizing that we must be kind to ourselves first, ensuring we're not depleted to the point of vulnerability to Satan's attacks. Jesus himself, despite his extraordinary acts of kindness, withdrew to pray and found strength from God the Father. This intentional self-care allowed him to perform the remarkable deeds of compassion and grace.

Understanding this delicate balance involves recognizing that an empty vessel cannot fill another. To pour out compassion, grace, and forgiveness to others in the right way and to keep ourselves from people's evil intentions, we must first fill ourselves with the wisdom and spirit of God. It's an art we refine as we spend more time in prayer and delve into God's Word, gradually mastering the ebb and flow of self-care and outward kindness.

In this journey of self-preparation and outreach, prayer emerges as the cornerstone. It is the constant, irrespective of external circumstances—health, sickness, joy, sadness, or worry. In his first letter to Thessalonians, Paul says, "Rejoice always, pray without ceasing, give thanks in all circumstances." (1 Thessalonians 5:16). Everyone, regardless of their beliefs, tends to reach out to something higher during tough or joyful times. Even people who don't follow a specific religion might express their thoughts or ask for help somehow. It's like an instinct in humans—to connect with something beyond ourselves. Whether asking for help or expressing thanks, this reaching out is a bit like a prayer. It's a way we all share in the human experience, showing our need for connection and meaning, regardless of our specific beliefs.

Sometimes, we might think that others who are not really into God need it more than those who already have a connection with God because they might be sicker or facing more significant problems. But it's super important to remember that, in God's eyes, we're all the same when needing his endless love and restoration.

So, as we balance caring for ourselves and helping others, let's make prayer our anchor. It's like a constant connection to God's love and strength. Whether we're feeling great or not-so-great, worried or happy, prayer is like a lifeline that keeps us connected to the extraordinary source of God's grace. It's a simple yet powerful act that reminds us that, in the grand scheme of things, we all need God's love and restoration. So let's keep praying and seeking forgiveness for the sins that we still tend to commit out of our sinful nature, though intentional or unintentional. And pray that we stay connected to the wellspring of God's boundless love and strength as we navigate the delicate balance of caring for ourselves and sharing that care with others.

Chapter 8

Cleanse Me

The idea of detoxification is frequently discussed within the health and wellness field. This is a methodical, scientific process in which the body eliminates pollutants to return to its ideal state. Similarly, the human spirit yearns for a thorough, spiritual purification beyond the physical. See it as a spiritual detox where the pollutants of stress, negativity, and unfinished business are released to make room for renewal. This chapter examines the science of spiritual cleansing and the transforming potential in the five-second prayer "God, Forgive me. Cleanse me. Make me whole again. Amen."

Yashoda Devi Ma, the creator of Modern Living Meditation and the Cosmic Women's Tribe, embodies the essence of cleansing in the world of spiritual learning. For her, spiritual cleansing is a set of exercises and behaviors intended to balance the complex relationship between the mind, body, soul, and spirit rather than just a ritual. The idea is to create an environment where negativity, toxicity, and pollutants are washed away, making a place for purity and spiritual clarity—much like the peaceful lake in the morning.

According to Yashoda Devi Ma, a spiritual cleanse is a conscious attempt to eliminate anything harmful from our lives. Her wise words, "What we observe, we become," such as the constant ingestion of stress, negativity, drama, and distractions from a world full of them, can wear us out on the mental, emotional, physical, and spiritual levels. It's a weight that steadily mounts up and impacts every aspect of our lives. "If our attention is always absorbed in stress, negativity, loss, drama, gossip, lack, comparison, competition, past, future, or ego, then our energy becomes low and weighs us mentally, emotionally, physically, and spiritually," says Yashoda Devi Ma. It's a significant insight that emphasizes our attention has an influence on our general well-being and its power.

From her point of view, not engaging in regular spiritual activities might result in energy stagnation, which can ensnare us in a negative cycle. If we don't consciously attempt to purify our spiritual selves, our energy is open to the effects of the outside world and absorbs whatever we focus on. This then impacts relationships, decision-making, and our capacity for happiness and fulfillment, which echoes throughout our existence.

Therefore, the cry for spiritual purification is also for liberation—a release from the weights that mount up in the daily grind. It is an invitation to submerge oneself in the waters of rebirth, parallel to rising from the waters of baptism or discovering peace following a storm. Spiritual cleansing's transformative power resides in its capacity to release us from the bonds of negativity, enabling us to emerge renewed and reborn into a world full of inner peace and spiritual clarity.

Everybody needs spiritual purification at some point in their life and even needs it again and again because we live in a world where Satan has power, and he is constantly after us to kill, steal, and destroy. Still, many of us may attribute these signals to the ups and downs of daily life or the demands of our daily grind. Restlessness becomes ordinary stress, echoes mere memories we think we've left behind, and heaviness is the cost of living in a fast-paced world. So how can we know whether it is merely a day-to-day grind or a call for spiritual cleansing?

Understanding that it's time for a spiritual cleanse is similar to experiencing a change in the breeze before a storm. Little clues in our behavior, health, and emotions prompt us to acknowledge the accumulation of spiritual weight. Remember that our body, mind, and spirit collaborate to convey these messages, serving as a personal road map for our spiritual journey. It manifests as occasional uneasiness or recurring internal tensions stemming from the past. A feeling of heaviness permeates our thoughts, similar to a shadow. Our spirit subtly indicates its own fatigue and yearns for a sense of liberation, much like our body alerts us when it is fatigued. It's tired; our spirit quietly hints at its own weariness, longing for liberation.

Discussed below are five key indicators that signal the necessity for a renewal of the spirit and offer insights into how Christians can embark on a transformative journey back to a place of spiritual vitality:

1. *You feel weighed down and exhausted.* As a Christian, feeling persistently weighed down and exhausted can indicate that your spiritual well-being needs attention. Despite receiving physical rest, a heavy heart and burdened spirit may linger. This exhaustion could manifest as a weariness of the soul, indicating that the cares of life have taken precedence over seeking God's rest and peace.

   One biblical example that vividly illustrates the concept of spiritual weariness is the story of the prophet Elijah on Mount Horeb, which is found in 1 Kings 19:1–18. After experiencing a great victory against the prophets of Baal, Elijah found himself fleeing for his life from the wrath of Queen Jezebel. Despite his triumph, the weight of fear and isolation burdened his spirit.

   Elijah's experience resonates with the feeling of being weighed down and exhausted as he sat under a broom tree, asking God to take his life. In this moment of despair, God provided physical rest and sustenance through an angel, showing that even the mightiest servants of God can experience moments of profound fatigue.

The Lord then directed Elijah to Mount Horeb, where a mighty wind, an earthquake, and fire passed by, but God was not in these dramatic displays. Instead, God spoke to Elijah in a gentle whisper. This event serves as a reminder that God's rest and renewal often come in quiet moments of intimate connection rather than grand displays of power.

2. *Swinging between emotional extremities.* Experiencing emotional extremes, ranging from numbness to oversensitivity may signify spiritual imbalance. Christians are called to be anchored in the love and grace of God, yet when emotions fluctuate dramatically, it can disrupt the spiritual equilibrium. It is important to seek emotional healing through prayer, surrender, and a renewed focus on God's unwavering promises.

King David's emotional life, as described in his psalms, offers a moving biblical illustration of the highs and lows that are a part of being human. David shares his heart in Psalm 13, revealing thoughts of hopelessness and abandonment. "How long, O Lord?" he asks, questioning God. "Will you always forget who I am?"" This sorrowful cry expresses various extreme emotions, from numbness to an intense sense of abandonment.

For Christians facing their own emotional anguish, David's openness to express the whole gamut of his emotions in the psalms provides a profound lesson.

Even though David goes through times of despair, he finally turns to prayer and surrenders to God. David transitions from mourning to trust in the last portion of Psalm 13, saying, "But I have trusted in your steadfast love; my heart shall rejoice in your salvation."

This biblical illustration demonstrates the transformational potential of pursuing emotional healing via a sincere, intimate relationship with God. Given that David was a man after God's heart, Christians experiencing extremes in their emotions can take comfort in his path. Believers can refocus on Scripture's unfailing promises of love, grace, and steadfast fellowship by admitting these emotions and giving them to God.

3. *Cycle of negativity.* Being enmeshed in a negative cycle, whether via deliberate effort or inadvertent creation, indicates a lack of connection with God and his love, joy, and peace. It is essential to realize that these thoughts are instead rooted in various ungodly things that grow in our hearts and minds due to our lack of proximity to Christ. Hence, it is crucial to break free from unfavorable habits and work toward establishing a mindset based on faith, forgiving others, and being grateful.

   The letter written by the apostle Paul to the Philippians offers a powerful scriptural illustration of how to deal with pessimism and develop a mindset based on faith.

Despite his incarceration, Paul exudes happiness and hope in his speech. He exhorts believers in Philippians 4:4–9 to always delight in the Lord, worry about nothing, and fix their thoughts on true, noble, just, pure, beautiful, and praiseworthy things. This chapter shows how Christians can purposefully turn their attention toward upbeat and pleasant thoughts, acting as a potent remedy against the vicious cycle of pessimism. Paul's emphasis on using appreciation and prayer as weapons against negativity is consistent with the transformational potential of gratitude. Selecting thankfulness releases the mind from the grip of negativity and focuses it on God's faithfulness and goodness.

Paul also emphasizes that forgiveness is important to preserving a loving and peaceful atmosphere. He advises "Let your gentleness be evident to all" in verse 5. The Lord is not far away." This awareness of God's closeness inspires Christians to let go of their grudges and complaints, creating a loving and compassionate environment that balances the negativity frequently rooted in unforgiveness.

4. *Straying from spiritual practices.* For many Christians, prayer, meditation, and studying Scripture are vital connections to God. If you ever neglect these practices or feel distant from your personal growth journey, consider it a gentle nudge for a spiritual reset. As advice, remember that intentionally embracing these spiritual disciplines can guide you back to a meaningful and

consistent relationship with God. The parable of the prodigal son, as told by Jesus in Luke 15:11–24, offers a powerful illustration of straying from one's spiritual practices and the subsequent return to a meaningful relationship with God. Initially desiring independence, the younger son squanders his inheritance in a distant country far from his father's house. In the midst of his wayward journey, he finds himself in dire circumstances, realizing the emptiness of a life apart from his family and, by extension, God.

This parable mirrors the experience of Christians who, over time, may drift away from essential spiritual practices. The prodigal son's realization that he was far from his father's love and provision serves as a poignant metaphor for believers who sense a spiritual void due to neglecting prayer, meditation, and the study of Scripture.

The turning point in the parable occurs when the prodigal son returns to his father's house, acknowledging his need for a restored relationship. Similarly, Christians who recognize the distance created by straying from spiritual practices can embark on a journey of return, seeking to reestablish a meaningful connection with God.

5. *Life happening to you, not for you.* Feeling as though life is happening to you, not for you, may signal a spiritual detachment. Instead of being a passive observer, consider this a prompt to reevaluate your perspective. Focus on surrendering to God's

control, trusting in his plans and time, and discerning purpose in every circumstance.

An insightful example of facing life's obstacles with faith can be found in Joseph's story. Joseph endured a string of misfortunes that may have easily led to resentment and hopelessness, including being sold into slavery by his envious brothers, being wrongly accused, and being imprisoned. But Joseph made a different decision. Speaking to his brothers, Joseph says in Genesis 50:20, "You meant to harm me, but God intended it for good to accomplish what is now being done, the saving of many lives." Joseph's story exemplifies the life-changing potential that results from submitting to God's plan, even in the face of seemingly insurmountable obstacles.

Joseph's journey inspires us to actively participate in God's unfolding plan rather than passively observe life's happenings. We can find meaning in any situation by putting our faith in his omnipotent control, even in the painful or unfair ones.

A road map for overcoming obstacles in life with faith and resiliency can be found by aligning our perspective with this biblical truth. Giving yourself to God's plan enables us to overcome hardship and embrace an outlook that recognizes his purpose amid life's complexity, just as Joseph's tale illustrates.

These signs are not the decrees of an external authority but rather the subtle whispers of your own inner being. In its wisdom, your spirit communicates through the language of emotions, energy, and the delicate balance of your inner landscape. Your intuition and self-awareness provide insight into these signs, guiding you toward a deeper understanding of your spiritual state. Consider these indicators as the spiritual barometer of your internal world. They are not imposed judgments but gentle signals urging you to pay attention to the needs of your soul.

Much like a computer overrun by viruses that constantly give pop-up messages on the screens, our spirits do the same. In those times, we need to understand that God sent Jesus to redeem our souls and return them to the way God intended them to be. Hence, we must not try to weigh ourselves down trying to understand complex computer codes because that is not our task; our task is to reboot and let God run the algorithms to bring us a state he intended for us, which was corrupted, similar to returning a computer to its original factory settings that its creator intended it to be in.

When God purifies our hearts and releases us to experience his presence, he does it in a wholesome manner that is lasting and not a quick fix. It's a process that enables us to enter and experience the purposes for which God made us by helping us see our infinite value and worth. Life can rapidly feel twisted and confusing when our souls are not functioning as intended, much like the frustration of trying to use a faulty computer that contains the core of our lives.

We should be grateful in soul-cleansing moments; we experience the shaking of our conscience and spirit by the Spirit of the Lord. This divine intervention helps us shed the burdens, the complexities, and the entanglements that hinder our journey. We should be thankful for this shaking, for it is the loving hand of God at work, guiding us back to the purity of heart and purpose for which we were originally intended.

The road never truly ends after cleansing. Instead, it encourages us to always live in God's presence. Our mended spirits flourish when we are in our Creator's tender, transforming presence, just as a repaired computer performs best in its original setting. We embark on a new chapter, led by the love of God, and experience the fullness of the life he planned for us as we let go of the entanglements of our past.

Make Me Whole Again

As we soak in the powerful feeling of being cleansed, remember that this incredible journey doesn't stop at forgiveness. Being forgiven is like being freed from a huge debt that is impossible to pay off, lifted by Christ's kindness. With forgiveness, a gentle breeze of renewal wafts into our souls and minds—an experience intricately entwined with the presence of God's Spirit.

But the story does not end with that debt disappearing or momentarily experiencing freedom and lightness through the Spirit of God. Instead, they are an opportunity to live a wholesome life as long as we live. In simpler terms, it marks the beginning of a journey to slowly repair the parts of ourselves damaged by our mistakes hand in hand with God—a journey toward becoming whole again.

You must have heard the famous saying, "God helps those who help themselves." While I am not an avid believer of this saying, I cannot deny that there is some truth to it. In James 4:8, James writes, *"Draw near to God, and He will draw near to you,"* implying that you must take the initiative for God to draw near to you. Remember that the dissymmetry of our souls cannot be mended by any other means than God, our Creator and King. Once he breaks off the shackles, submit to him and follow him with all your heart, soul, and mind.

I recall these powerful words from an unknown author who stayed with me: *"Sanctification is not an event; it is a process."* It's a reminder that the result of being forgiven or cleansed by the blood of the Lamb isn't a sudden, overnight transformation. Sometimes, we misunderstand what it means to receive forgiveness. We might think that once we have been forgiven, we are instantly a wholly new and changed person. But that is different from how it works. It is not about a sudden, dramatic shift. Instead, we are given a gift—a new nature, a fresh perspective, a different approach, and a renewed spirit. These are the building blocks for creating a new life that's truly worth living for Christ.

So, technically, forgiveness is the starting point, the catalyst for this ongoing process of becoming more aligned with Christ's teachings. It is the saving of our lives from the eternal fire of hell that is accomplished in that one-time event when we accept Christ as our Savior and oath to spend the rest of our lives with him. The second part is where we gradually embrace this newfound nature and let it shape our thoughts, actions, and overall outlook. Day by day, step by step, we align ourselves more closely with the values of Christ, making our lives a testament to the transformative power of his grace and mercy. This is what I mean when I say "whole again."

In the Gospel of Matthew 7:7–8, there is a profound lesson: *"Ask, and it will be given to you; seek, and you will find; knock and the door will be opened to you. For everyone who asks receives; the one who seeks finds; and to the one who knocks, the door will be opened."* It teaches us that while God generously gives, there's a condition—asking and seeking.

This applies particularly to personal requests and special favors, not just the universal blessings like the sun and rain. The beauty lies in that when we ask from God, unlike with people, there's no disappointment for those who trust and ask in faith. So, after that transformative reset, much like a factory reset, instead of relying solely on people and expecting their help on your journey to firming up your faith, lean on God and carefully choose genuine friends, family, or a mentor.

Underestimating this initial phase can be detrimental, akin to the seeds falling on the roadside or among thorns. Investing effort in experiencing the fullness of the goodness God has in store for us is crucial. It goes beyond merely expressing gratitude for forgiveness; it's about actively engaging with the transformative process.

Walking this road requires commitment, prayer, and persistence in asking God to guide us to become "whole again." I must warn you that it is a challenging process. It is not an easy walk, but the encouraging part is that it is a team effort between us trying hard and God's power making it happen. As we go along, we're open to the opportunities God gives us, playing an active part in our complete restoration.

The Word of God is filled with stories that witness the transformative power of God's grace, the efficacy of prayer, and the collaborative effort between human endeavor and divine intervention in the process of restoration. The story of the prodigal son, as recorded in the Gospel of Luke 15:11–32 is worth mentioning.

The careless son of a king ends up in a terrible situation as he leaves his house and spends his inheritance carelessly. After realizing his poor condition and that all his money is wasted, he decides to go back home, hoping to be a mere servant since he does not think he is longer worthy to be called the king's son. However, the father's answer is a metaphor for God's unending grace. The son is praised rather than chastised since he is eager to make amends and is sorry. His relationship with his father is fully restored. Had the father not made him whole again, he would have let him become his mere servant. But that is not God's nature, after all. God's grace restores us completely.

The parable of the lost son stands as a timeless story of the power of team effort, capturing the profound insights and actions of the son and the unwavering acceptance and redemption offered by his father. This story gives us a valuable lesson and instills a sense of hope within us.

It serves as a moving reminder that even when we stray from our destined path, there is always a way back to the embrace of the Father. As I highlighted earlier, the journey will not be easy; the temptations and worldly desires of the flesh can weaken us. There will be instances when, out of weakness, we might feel that we will fall again, and on occasion, we will succumb to sin. But remember that the Holy Spirit is our guide and that through the sacrifice of Christ, we have been made righteous with God.

Recalling this righteousness in times of stumbling and spiritual weakness, rise again and run toward God. The righteous may fall seven times but rise again because the Lord is their hope. This parable encourages us to persevere, recognize our inherent worthiness through divine grace, and find solace in unconditional love and forgiveness because it's not just about God magically fixing everything; instead, it's a collaborative effort.

You have found a source of inner inspiration when you realize that you have been made righteous with Christ. It's not simply a truth you must accept; it's a motivating factor that helps you continue. Envision a withering tree that has undergone restoration and pruning. The tree's fruits are a reliable gauge of its level of recovery. Analogously, seeing our righteousness in Christ is the impetus for manifesting righteousness in our lives.

Just as the outward signs of a healthy tree reveal its restoration, the fruits of righteousness in our actions and attitudes become visible markers of our internal transformation. The change within us starts reflecting in how we treat others, the kindness we show, and the love we extend. This external manifestation becomes a testament to the profound work happening within us.

So, as you work on your internal faith and connection with God, it's time to let that transformative power produce visible fruits of goodness. Just as a restored tree displays vibrant and thriving fruits, your life can become a testimony to the restoration and change that can encourage others to seek the light. In the Gospel of Matthew 5:15–16, Christ says, *"Neither do people light a lamp and put it under a bowl. Instead, they put it on its stand, giving everyone in the house light. In the same way, let your light shine before others, that they may see your good deeds and glorify your Father in heaven."* It's not just about personal growth; it's about sharing your newfound identity in Christ with others to give glory to our Father in heaven.

So, as much as you can, allow the love, grace, and righteousness you've received from Christ to flow into your actions for others. "*You received without payment; give without payment,*" (Matthew 10:8). When others witness the favorable fruits in your life, they see a living testimony of the transformative power of God's love.

Here are a few tangible ways to recognize that something profound has changed within you; it's like signals of the inward transformation becoming visible in your actions and demeanor:

1. *Change in habits.* One noticeable sign is when you give up habits inconsistent with your newfound commitment to a godly life. Whether it's quitting harmful addictions such as overcoming a dependence on substances like cigarettes or breaking free from the grip of alcohol, abandoning unwholesome entertainment choices like choosing to no longer indulge in content that promotes negativity or goes against your values, or breaking free from negative thought patterns, such as overcoming persistent self-doubt or pessimism, is a powerful manifestation of your internal change.

2. *Becoming an ambassador of Christ.* As you grow in your faith, you naturally become an ambassador of Christ. This means your words and actions increasingly reflect the values and teachings of Jesus and the fruits of the Holy Spirit. Your conversations might revolve around love, compassion, and forgiveness. People will notice that you actively seek to emulate Christ in your interactions, promoting a positive and uplifting atmosphere.

3. *Transformation in dress and appearance.* Another practical example of reflecting

change in your life could involve your way of dressing or personal appearance. It's not necessarily about adhering to a strict dress code but a visible transformation that signifies a more profound shift within—more reflective of the God you serve.

For instance, consider a scenario where someone favored visibly more revealing clothes or cosmetic surgery. In the process of internal change, they might prefer more modest attire and or appearance. This shift is not merely about covering the body but reflects a newfound modesty, simplicity, or purposefulness in presenting themselves to the world. The change becomes a tangible expression of their internal transformation, echoing the commitment to a more aligned and purposeful life.

4. *Altered treatment of others.* How you treat people is a compelling indicator of your spiritual growth, extending beyond kindness, empathy, and patience. A truly transformed heart embraces the challenging principle of loving even your enemies and extending kindness to the poor and lowly. This depth of compassion is reflected in actions like praying for them even when they hurt or cause you harm, going out of your way to help others, offering a listening ear, and genuinely caring for their well-being. Others will notice the authenticity and sincerity in your interactions, mirroring the profound transformation Christ has caused in your life.

5. *Shift in priorities.* When your priorities shift towards spiritual matters, it becomes

evident in the way you allocate your time, resources, and energy. This transformation is tangible through various expressions, such as dedicating substantial time to prayer and meditation, engaging in religious, faith-based, or community activities during leisure time, and investing in spiritual education to deepen your understanding. Additionally, your social circle may evolve to include like-minded individuals who share your spiritual values, and your energy might be redirected from relentless material pursuits to selflessly serving others. This reallocation reflects a profound commitment to nurturing your spiritual well-being and contributing positively to your spiritual community and the broader world.

As you grow in your faith, these changes become natural expressions of the power of God's grace working within you. While not everyone may recognize these shifts immediately, these visible signs testify to the journey from being cleansed to becoming *whole again*.

Conclusion

As the different facets of the transforming journey—a journey of self-discovery, connection, and restoration—that we went through in the book's chapters come to a close, we find ourselves here again reciting the five-second prayer, *"Forgive me. Cleanse me. Make me whole again. Amen."* In our present invocation, our prayer is not rooted in ignorance of its potency; instead, we have fully grasped and internalized the profound efficacy and transformative influence that this prayer holds for our lives. Above all, it is a five-second complete package, perhaps like a potion that connects us with the Heavenly Father, immediately drawing us closer to him in every possible way in any given situation.

Remember that we now have a clear road map that equips us with all the information we need to navigate our spiritual journey. We also have the required tools, which are prayer and the Word of God. We have the guide—the Holy Spirit—and we are well aware of the possible traps and tricks and know how to deal with them. Unsurprisingly, our sins, which are washed by the blood of the Lamb, are the devil's most excellent trap to hinder our growth. He loves to reshow them to us to continue to inflict guilt and keep us from making any advancements. But we know what God said, right? *"Come now, let us reason together, says the Lord: though your sins are like scarlet, they shall be as white as snow; though they are red like crimson, they shall become like wool"* (Isaiah 1:18).

Paradoxically, notions such as forgiveness, restoration, redemption, and atonement are frequently envisioned unfolding in grandiose and monumental settings. Ironically, reality often paints a different picture. Even during the time of Jesus, the Jewish community antici-pated a Messiah who would bring about physical salvation, liberating them from Roman oppression, often envisioning a triumphant figure wielding swords in a grand spectacle.

However, Jesus's plan diverged from these expectations. Rather than orchestrating a dramatic and forceful liberation, his teachings emphasized love, compassion, and a profound transformation of the human heart. In his vision, the Messiah wasn't about wielding swords against political adversaries but about a spiritual revolution that tran-scended conventional expectations.

This departure from the anticipated grandeur serves as a poi-gnant reminder that the most remarkable works sometimes unfold themselves in the most organic and ordinary ways. The transforma-tive power of forgiveness, restoration, redemption, and atonement often emerges quietly, touching lives in subtle and understated ways, transcending the grandiose expectations that may initially surround them. It underscores the profound truth that the extraordinary can be found in the simplicity of everyday moments, demonstrating that the impact of these phenomena transcends the need for flashy displays.

This contradictory fact is in line with my own path. There were times in my life when there was no denying the difference between what I did and what God wanted. I became involved in practices and pursuits that were at odds with his teachings and continued them even though I knew they offended him. My spirit finally became weary of defending these acts, and I gave up on his divine purpose for my life.

This story took a dramatic turn when I faced the fact that some-one I employed—someone I thought was my sister—was a thief and a liar. I used to continually find ways to rationalize and defend her acts, even after years of deceit and stealing, which left me feeling deeply guilty. The turning point was reached when something hap-pened that defied explanation in every way. I realized it was time to give God the situation and her because of an indisputable sin.

I started my path of seeking forgiveness in the silent place of prayer by humbly pleading for my own forgiveness. Realizing I had been a willing participant in her behavior, I prayed to God to purify my thoughts and instill a new spirit. It was challenging to let her leave my company and my life since she had become more than just an employee; she had become a sister. Still, I had to make a change after realizing that my salvation was at serious risk. I recalled what Jesus said in Matthew 5:29, *"If your right eye causes you to sin, tear it out and throw it away. For you should lose one of your members than that your whole body be thrown into hell."*

This simple story highlights how ordinary situations can bring about significant changes, similar to the unexpected twists in the bigger story of redemption. Asking for forgiveness started a transformation, showing that redemption can be a mix of admitting mistakes and wanting to change. In the essential act of apologizing and forgiving, something exceptional happens in regular moments. It's a reminder that redemption often occurs quietly without needing flashy displays.

As we continue the journey of restoration, the realization dawns that it's not only the monumental sins that bind us but the everyday struggles and shortcomings that also entangle our spirits. Once redeemed from the clutches of spiritual death, the ongoing challenge lies in freeing ourselves from the shackles of daily transgressions. In the quiet moments of self-reflection, we confront the mundane sins that threaten to weigh down our souls. These are the ordinary struggles, the habitual shortcomings, and the daily choices that align us closer to God's teachings or lead us astray.

When we ask for forgiveness for big or small mistakes, we learn that redemption isn't some far-off goal but a daily road. It's a journey where each step and apology helps free our soul bit by bit. Understanding this, we see that the profound grace of redemption touches every part of our lives, turning the extraordinary into something we can find in the simplicity of our everyday decisions.

As we conclude this journey together, exploring the profound realms of forgiveness, atonement, and the resonating power encapsulated in the five-second prayer, I extend an invitation to commit. This marks the commencement of actively integrating salvation into our lives' very essence.

Now, armed with the wisdom gleaned from these pages, it's time to step into the arena of your own existence and actively partake in the ongoing narrative of redemption. Embrace the five-second prayer as a constant companion, a bridge connecting the vast expanse between your shortcomings and the boundless grace of God. Let it be the beacon that guides you through the labyrinth of everyday choices, whispering the path to redemption in every decision you make.

But don't let this journey be solitary. Share your redemption stories with others. Be a testament to the transformative power of forgiveness, a living embodiment of the five-second prayer's influence in your life. Your narrative has the potential to kindle hope in the hearts of those grappling with their own struggles, sparking a chain reaction of redemption within your community.

In your circles, be a source of inspiration. Extend a hand of compassion to those burdened by guilt and despair, introducing them to the liberating embrace of forgiveness. Encourage the practice of the five-second prayer as a simple yet profound tool for connecting with God in the midst of life's chaos.

Let your journey become a ripple that transforms the currents of those around you. Remember, redemption isn't a solitary endeavor; it's a communal pilgrimage where we uplift one another toward the light of divine grace. So, as you step forth from these pages, carry with you the torch of salvation, igniting a flame of hope in the hearts of those who yearn for renewal. Embrace the call to action, not merely as a conclusion but as the commencement of a shared journey toward a life redeemed and a spirit rekindled.

Amen.

A Personalized Prayer Journal

96 Verses and Self-Reflections
The following verses were used throughout this book.
Reflect on how each one can impact your prayer journey.

"To whom much is given, much is required!" (Luke 12:48).

____
____
____
____

"But when you pray, go into your room, close the door, and pray to your Father, who is unseen" (Matthew 6:6).

____
____
____
____

"Call to me, and I will answer you and tell you great and unsearchable things you do not know" (Jeremiah 33:3).

____
____
____
____

"After the earthquake came a fire, but the Lord was not in the fire. And after the fire came to a gentle whisper" (1 Kings 19:12).

"Paul and his companions traveled throughout the region of Phrygia and Galatia, having been kept by the Holy Spirit from preaching the word in the province of Asia. When they came to the border of Mysia, they tried to enter Bithynia, but the Spirit of Jesus would not allow them to" (Acts 16:6–7).

"The LORD is my shepherd; I shall not want. He made me lie down in green pastures and leadeth me beside the still waters. He restoreth my soul: he leadeth me in the paths of righteousness for his name's sake. Yea, though I walk through the valley of the shadow of death, I will fear no evil: for thou art with me; thy rod and thy staff comfort me. Thou preparest a table before me in the presence of my enemies: thou anoint my head with oil; my cup runs over. Surely goodness and mercy shall follow me all the days of my life: and I will dwell in the house of the LORD forever" (Psalm 23).

"But the Lord said to Samuel, 'Do not consider his appearance or height, for I have rejected him. The Lord does not look at the things people look at. People look at the outward appearance, but the Lord looks at the heart" (1 Samuel 16:7).

"O come, let us worship and bow down: kneel before the Lord our maker" (Psalm 95:6).

"Be careful of nothing, but in everything by prayer and supplication with thanksgiving let your requests be made known unto God" (Philippians 4:6).

"I exhort therefore, that, first of all, supplications, prayers, intercessions, and giving of thanks, be made for all men" (1 Timothy 2:1).

"Nothing in all creation is hidden from God's sight" (Hebrews 4:13).

"Does as He pleases with the powers of heaven and the peoples of the earth" (Daniel 4:35).

"The Lord is good, and His love endures forever" (Psalm 100:5).

"Ask, and it will be given to you; seek, and you will find; knock, and the door will be opened to you" (Matthew 7:7).

"Have faith in God…whatever you ask for in prayer, believe that you have received it, and it will be yours" (Mark 11:22, 24).

"This kind can come out only by prayer" (Mark 9:29).

"Get up and pray so you will not succumb to temptation" (Luke 22:46).

"If you believe, you will receive whatever you ask for in prayer" (Matthew 21:22).

"They should always pray and not give up" (Luke 18:1).

"And I will do whatever you ask in my name, so that the Father may be glorified. You may ask me for anything in my name, and I will do it" (John 14:13–14).

"Pray also for me, that whenever I speak, words may be given me so that I will fearlessly make known the mystery of the gospel" (Ephesians 6:19).

"At the same time, pray also for us, that God may open to us a door for the word, to declare the mystery of Christ, on account of which I am in" (Colossians 4:3–4).

"Finally, brethren, pray for us, that the word of the Lord may have free course, and be glorified, even as it is with you: and that we may be delivered from unreasonable and wicked men: for all men have not faith" (2 Thessalonians 3:1–2).

"For I know that this shall turn to my salvation through your prayer and the supply of the Spirit of Jesus Christ" (Philippians 1:19).

"But we will give ourselves continually to prayer and the ministry of the word" (Acts 6:4).

"Confess your faults one to another, and pray one for another, that ye may be healed. The effectual fervent prayer of a righteous man availed much. Elias was a man subject to like passions as we are, and he prayed earnestly that it might not rain, and it rained not on the earth by the space of three years and six months. And he prayed again, and the heavens gave rain, and the earth brought forth her fruit" (James 5:16–18).

"Thy kingdom come, Thy will be done in earth, as it is in heaven" (Matthew 6:10).

"Trust in the Lord with all of your heart; and lean not unto your own understanding. In all thy ways, acknowledge Him, and He will make our paths straight" (Proverbs 3:5–6).

"If any of you lack wisdom, let him ask of God, that giveth to all men liberally, and unbraided not; and it shall be given him" (James 1:5).

"I can do all things through Him who gives me strength" (Philippians 4:13).

"Now, when Daniel learned that the decree had been published, he went home to his upstairs room, where the windows opened toward Jerusalem. Three times a day, he knelt and prayed, giving thanks to his God, just as he had done before" (Daniel 6:10).

"Have mercy on me, O God, according to your unfailing love; according to your great compassion, blot out my transgressions. Wash away all my iniquity and cleanse me of my sins" (Psalm 51).

"Now, on his way to Jerusalem, Jesus traveled along the border between Samaria and Galilee. As he was going into a village, ten men who had leprosy met him. They stood at a distance and called out in a loud voice, 'Jesus, Master, pity us!' When he saw them, he said, 'Go, show yourselves to the priests.' And as they went, they were cleansed. One of them, when he saw he was healed, came back, praising God in a loud voice. He threw himself at Jesus' feet and thanked him—and he was a

Samaritan. Jesus asked, 'Were not all ten cleansed? Where are the other nine? Has no one returned to give praise to God except this foreigner?' Then he said to him, 'Rise and go; your faith has made you well'" (Luke 17:11–19).

"At Gibeon, the Lord appeared to Solomon during the night in a dream, and God said, 'Ask for whatever you want me to give you…So, give your servant a discerning heart to govern your people and to distinguish between right and wrong. For who can govern this great people of yours?…And if you obey me and keep my decrees and commands as David, your father did, I will give you a long life" (1 Kings 3:5–14).

"Two men went up to the temple to pray, one a Pharisee and the other a tax collector. The Pharisee stood by himself and prayed: God, I thank you that I am not like other people—robbers, evildoers, adulterers—or even like this tax collector. I fast twice a week and give a tenth of all I get. But the tax collector stood at a distance. He would not even look up to heaven but beat his breast and said, 'God, have mercy on me, a sinner.' I tell you that this man, rather than the other, went home justified before God. All those who exalt themselves will be humbled, and those who humble themselves will be exalted" (Luke 18:9–14).

"When the day of Pentecost came, they were all together in one place. Suddenly, a sound like the blowing of a violent wind came from heaven and filled the whole house where they were sitting. They saw what

seemed to be tongues of fire that separated and came to rest on each of them. All of them were filled with the Holy Spirit and began to speak in other tongues as the Spirit enabled them" (Acts 2:1–4).

____

____

____

____

"So, they took away the stone. Then Jesus looked up and said, 'Father, I thank you that you have heard me. I knew that you always hear me, but I said this to benefit the people standing here, that they may believe that you sent me'" (John 11:41–42).

____

____

____

____

____

____

"About midnight, Paul and Silas were praying and singing hymns to God, and the other prisoners were listening to them. Suddenly, there was such a violent earthquake that the foundations of the prison were shaken. All the prison doors flew open at once, and everyone's chains came loose" (Acts 16:25–26).

____

____

____

____

"And a woman was there who had been subject to bleeding for twelve years. She had suffered a great deal under the care of many doctors and had spent all she had, yet instead of getting better, she grew worse. When she heard about Jesus, she came up behind him in the crowd and touched his cloak because she thought, If I just touched his clothes, I will be healed. Immediately, her bleeding stopped, and she felt in her body that she was freed from her suffering. At once, Jesus realized that power had gone out of him. He turned around in the crowd and asked,

'Who touched my clothes?' 'You see the people crowding against you,' his disciples answered, 'and yet you can ask, "Who touched me?"' But Jesus kept looking around to see who had done it. Then the woman, knowing what had happened to her, came and fell at his feet and, trembling with fear, told him the whole truth. He said to her, 'Daughter, your faith has healed you. Go in peace and be freed from your suffering'" (Mark 5:25–34).

____

____

____

"Someone touched me: I know that power has left me" (Luke 8:46).

____

____

____

"For it is with your heart that you believe and are justified, and it is with your mouth that you profess your faith and are saved" (Romans 10:10).

____

____

____

"I am the true vine, and my father is the vinedresser. Every branch in me that does not bear fruit he takes away, and every branch that does bear fruit he prunes that it may bear more fruit" (John 15:1).

____

____

____

"Bear one another's burdens, and so fulfill the law of Christ" (Galatians 6:2).

____

____

____

"Let us then approach God's throne of grace with confidence so that we may receive mercy and find grace to help us in our time of need" (Hebrews 4:16).

____
____
____
____

"Cast all your anxiety on Him because He cares for you" (1 Peter 5:7).

____
____
____
____

"This poor man cried, and the Lord heard him and saved him from all his troubles" (Psalm 34).

____
____
____
____

"Look to the Lord and His strength; seek His face always" (Psalm 105:4).

____
____
____
____

"Search us, God, and know our hearts; test us and know our anxious thoughts. See if there is any offensive way in us and lead us in the way everlasting" (Psalm 139:23–24).

____
____
____
____

"Then the Lord appeared to Abram and said, 'To your offspring, I will give this land.' So, he built there an altar to the Lord, who had appeared to him" (Genesis 12:7).

"So Abram moved his tent and settled by the oaks of Mamre, which are at Hebron, and there he built an altar to the Lord" (Genesis 13:18).

"Moses used to take the tent and pitch it outside the camp, far off from the camp, and he called it the tent of meeting. And everyone who sought the Lord would go out to the tent of meeting outside the camp" (Exodus 33:7–11).

"Hearing that Jesus had silenced the Sadducees, the Pharisees got together. One of them, an expert in the law, tested him with this question: Teacher, which is the greatest commandment in the Law? Jesus replied: 'Love the Lord your God with all your heart, soul, and mind.' This is the first and greatest commandment. And the second is like it: 'Love your neighbor as yourself.' All the Law and the Prophets hang on these two commandments" (Matthew 22:34–40).

"Then Jesus went with his disciples to a place called Gethsemane, and he said to them, 'Sit here while I go over there and pray.' He took Peter and the two sons of Zebedee along with him, and he began to be sorrowful and troubled. Then he said to them, 'My soul is overwhelmed with sorrow to the point of death. Stay here and keep watch with me.' Going a little farther, he fell with his face to the ground and prayed, 'My Father, if it is possible, may this cup be taken from me. Yet not as I will, but as you will.' Then, he returned to his disciples and found them sleeping. 'Couldn't you men keep watch with me for one hour?' he asked Peter. 'Watch and pray so that you will not fall into temptation. The spirit is willing, but the flesh is weak.' He went away a second time and prayed, 'My Father if this cup can't be taken away unless I drink it, may your will be done.' When he came back, he again found them sleeping because their eyes were heavy. So, he left them, went away once more, and prayed the third time, saying the same thing. Then he returned to the disciples and said, 'Are you still sleeping and resting? Look, the hour has come, and the Son of Man is delivered into the hands of sinners. Rise! Let us go! Here comes my betrayer!'" (Matthew 26:36–46).

____

____

____

"Father, if you are willing, take this cup from me; yet not my will, but yours be done" (Luke 22:42).

____

____

____

"Jesus went to the Mount of Olives as usual, and his disciples followed him. On reaching the place, he said to them, 'Pray that you will not fall into temptation.' He withdrew about a stone's throw beyond them, knelt, and prayed, 'Father, if you are willing, take this cup from me; yet not my will, but yours be done.' An angel from heaven appeared to him and strengthened him. And being in anguish, he prayed more earnestly,

and his sweat was like drops of blood falling to the ground. When he rose from prayer and returned to the disciples, he found them asleep, exhausted from sorrow. 'Why are you sleeping?' he asked them. 'Get up and pray so that you will not fall into temptation'" (Luke 22:39–46).

____

____

____

"About noon the following day, as they were on their journey and approaching the city, Peter went up on the roof to pray. He became hungry and wanted something to eat, and while the meal was being prepared, he fell into a trance. He saw heaven open, like a large sheet being let down to earth by its four corners. It contained all kinds of four-footed animals, reptiles, and birds. Then a voice told him, 'Get up, Peter. Kill and eat.' 'Surely not, Lord!' Peter replied. 'I have never eaten anything impure or unclean.' Again, the voice spoke to him, 'Do not call anything impure that God has made clean.' This happened three times, and immediately the sheet was returned to heaven. While Peter was wondering about the meaning of the vision, the men sent by Cornelius found out where Simon's house was and stopped at the gate. They called out, asking if Simon, who was known as Peter, was staying there. While Peter was still thinking about the vision, the Spirit said to him, 'Simon, three men are looking for you. So, get up and go downstairs. Do not hesitate to go with them, for I have sent them.' Peter went down and said to the men, 'I'm the one you're looking for. Why have you come?' The men replied, 'We have come from Cornelius the centurion. He is a righteous and God-fearing man who is respected by all the Jewish people. A holy angel told him to ask you to come to his house so that he could hear what you have to say.' Then Peter invited the men into the house to be his guests" (Acts 10:9–23).

____

____

____

"Where can I go from your Spirit? Where can I flee from your presence? If I go up to the heavens, you are there; if I make my bed in the depths, you are there. If I rise on the wings of the dawn, if I settle on the far side of the sea, even there, your hand will guide me; your right hand will hold me fast" (Psalm 139:7–10).

____

____

____

____

"For where two or three gather in my name, I am with them" (Matthew 18:20).

____

____

____

____

"By day, the Lord directs his love; at night, his song is with me—a prayer to the God of my life" (Psalm 42:8).

____

____

____

____

"Do not be anxious about anything, but in every situation, by prayer and petition, with thanksgiving, present your requests to God. And the peace of God, which transcends all understanding, will guard your hearts and minds in Christ Jesus" (Philippians 4:6–7).

____

____

____

____

"Pray continually" (1 Thessalonians 5:17).

____

____

____

"Your Father knows what you need before you ask him" (Matthew 6:8).

"This, then, is how you should pray: 'Our Father in heaven, hallowed be your name, your kingdom come, you will be done, on earth as it is in heaven. Give us today our daily bread. And forgive us our debts, as we also have forgiven our debtors. And lead us not into temptation, but deliver us from the evil one'" (Matthew 9:13).

"The heart is deceitful above all things and beyond cure. Who can understand it? The LORD *search the heart and examine the mind, to reward each person according to their conduct, according to what their deeds deserve"* (Jeremiah 17:9–10).

"The LORD *came and stood there, calling as at the other times, 'Samuel! Samuel!' Then Samuel said, 'Speak, for your servant is listening'"* (1 Samuel 3:10).

"In the morning, LORD, you hear my voice; in the morning, I lay my requests before you and wait expectantly" (Psalm 5:3).

____

____

____

____

"If we confess our sins, he is faithful and just and will forgive us and purify us from all unrighteousness" (1 John 1:9).

____

____

____

____

"I will set out and go back to my father and say to him: 'Father, I have sinned against heaven and you. I am no longer worthy to be called your son; make me like one of your hired servants.' So, he got up and went to his father. But while he was still a long way off, his father saw him and was filled with compassion for him; he ran to his son, threw his arms around him, and kissed him. The son said, 'Father, I have sinned against heaven and you. I am no longer worthy to be called your son" (Luke 15:18–21).

____

____

____

____

"And he directed the people to sit down on the grass. Taking the five loaves and the two fish and looking up to heaven, he gave thanks and broke the loaves. Then he gave them to the disciples, and the disciples gave them to the people" (Matthew 14:19).

____

____

____

____

"I have not stopped giving thanks for you, remembering you in my prayers. I keep asking that the God of our Lord Jesus Christ, the glorious Father, may give you the Spirit of wisdom and revelation so that you may know him better. I pray that the eyes of your heart may be enlightened so that you may know the hope he has called you, the riches of his glorious inheritance in his holy people" (Ephesians 1:16–18).

____

____

____

"Therefore, confess your sins to each other and pray for each other so that you may be healed. The prayer of a righteous person is powerful and effective" (James 5:16).

____

____

____

"For all have sinned and come short of the glory of God" (Romans 3:23).

____

____

____

"All are justified freely by his grace through the redemption that came by Christ Jesus" (Romans 3:24).

____

____

____

"But he said to me, 'My grace is sufficient for you, for my power is made perfect in weakness.' Therefore, I will boast all the more gladly about my weaknesses so that Christ's power may rest on me" (2 Corinthians 12:9).

____

____

____

"God demonstrates his own love for us in this: While we were still sinners, Christ died for us" (Romans 5:8).

"Jesus said to him, 'Receive your sight; your faith has healed you'" (Luke 18:42).

"To some who were confident of their own righteousness and looked down on everyone else, Jesus told this parable: 'Two men went up to the temple to pray, one a Pharisee and the other a tax collector. The Pharisee stood by himself and prayed: "God, I thank you that I am not like other people—robbers, evildoers, adulterers—or even like this tax collector. I fast twice a week and give a tenth of all I get." But the tax collector stood at a distance. He would not even look up to heaven but beat his breast and said, "God, have mercy on me, a sinner." I tell you that this man, rather than the other, went home justified before God. All those who exalt themselves will be humbled, and those who humble themselves will be exalted'" (Luke 18:9–14).

"Why do you look at the speck of sawdust in your brother's eye and pay no attention to the plank in your own eye? How can you say to your brother, 'Let me take the speck out of your eye,' when there is always a plank in your own eye? You hypocrite, first take the plank out of your own eye, and then you will see clearly to remove the speck from your brother's eye" (Matthew 7:3–5).

"Rejoice always" (1 Thessalonians 5:16).

"How long, LORD? Will you forget me forever? How long will you hide your face from me? How long must I wrestle with my thoughts and have sorrow in my heart day after day? How long will my enemy triumph over me? Look on me and answer, LORD my God. Give light to my eyes, or I will sleep in death, and my enemy will say, 'I have overcome him,' and my foes will rejoice when I fall.' But I trust in your unfailing love; my heart rejoices in your salvation. I will sing the LORD's praise, for he has been good to me" (Psalm 13).

"Rejoice in the Lord always. I will say it again: Rejoice! Let your gentleness be evident to all. The Lord is nearby. Do not be anxious about anything, but in every situation, by prayer and petition, with thanksgiving, present your requests to God. And the peace of God, which transcends all understanding, will guard your hearts and minds in Christ Jesus. Finally, brothers and sisters, whatever is true, whatever is noble, whatever is right, whatever is pure, whatever is lovely, whatever is admirable—if anything is excellent or praiseworthy—think about such things. Whatever you have learned, received, heard, or seen in me—put it into practice. And the God of peace will be with you" (Philippians 4:4–9).

"You intended to harm me, but God intended it for good to accomplish what is now being done, the saving of many lives" (Genesis 50:20).

"Come near to God and he will come near to you. Wash your hands, you sinners, and purify your hearts, you double-minded" (James 4:8).

"Ask, and it will be given to you; seek, and you will find; knock and the door will be opened to you. For everyone who asks receives; the one who seeks finds; and to the one who knocks, the door will be opened" (Matthew 7:7–8).

"Neither do people light a lamp and put it under a bowl. Instead, they put it on its stand, giving everyone in the house light. In the same way, let your light shine before others, that they may see your good deeds and glorify your Father in heaven" (Matthew 5:15–16).

"Heal the sick, raise the dead, cleanse those who have leprosy, drive out demons. Freely you have received; freely give" (Matthew 10:8).

<table>
<tr><td>

"Come now, let us reason together, says the Lord: though your sins are like scarlet, they shall be as white as snow; though they are red like crimson, they shall become like wool" (Isaiah 1:1).

____

____

____

____

"If your right eye causes you to sin, tear it out and throw it away. For it is better that you lose one of your members than that your whole body be thrown into hell" (Matthew 5:29).

____

____

____

____

</td></tr>
</table>

God, forgive me.
Cleanse me.
Make me whole again.
Amen.

About the Author

Dr. Ella L. Gates-Mahmoud

Dr. Ella L. Gates-Mahmoud resides in Minneapolis, Minnesota, where she serves as the executive director of a nonprofit educational organization. She founded Seed Academy Preschool in 1985 and Harvest Preparatory School in 1992, which are two of Minnesota's premiere educational institutions. Ella holds a bachelor's and master's degrees in organizational management and a doctorate degree in educational leadership and is a certified mediator trained at Hamline Law School as well as a Minnesota licensed school superintendent. She volunteered for over a decade as a guardian ad litem for Hennepin County Fourth Judicial Court. She was the first Black person to serve on the city of Minneapolis Charter Commission and worked as a newspaper reporter for two local historic Black newspapers. Ella is the 1982 Miss Black Minnesota and is married, has four adopted children, and was the legal guardian of a niece and goddaughter. Dr. Gates-Mahmoud is also the author of a children's book *Ebba's Knees Lock: Her Friends Call Her Ebonylocks* and has published her dissertation, *The Murder of George Floyd: A Case Study Examining How the Policing of Black Men and Grassroots Activism Influence the Will of Black Women to Lead,* on Concordia University–St. Paul, Minnesota, Digital Commons.